101 Quirks, Quips and Quotes

101 Quirks, Quips and Quotes

ᔆᕦ

Some of my crazy sayings, meaningful thoughts

and favorite Bible verses

Dan E. Perry

CHAPEL HILL
PRESS, INC.

This book is dedicated to my dear wife Margaret and our three children, Elizabeth, Daniel, Jr., and Radford, who frequently kid me about my many crazy expressions, and have challenged me to "write a book about them."

Seated in front of Margaret and Dan, left to right: Granddaughter Virginia (age 5), Radford, Daniel, Elizabeth, son-in-law Chad

CONTENTS

PART ONE

Some of My Crazy Sayings

1. Great Caesar's Ghost! Great Jumpin' Jehosaphat! 3
2. But I *like* burnt toast! 3
3. Don't worry about the mule goin' blind; you just load the cart! . . . 4
4. Let me show you a little trick I learned in the Roman Army many years ago. 4
5. Well I'll be jumped up and John dog my cats! 5
6. Do not worry, do not fret; just keep going without regret! 5
7. Sock-a-ma-roo-cha! Side-a-vays! 6
8. Aan-ya-haash-a-me-ka! Naan-aan-taan-sha-nul! Sala-haam-ne-da! Wa-ta-koo-she-wa! Aana-tao-aai-she-ma-su! *and* Wa-tah-shi . . . 7
9. Don't worry, I'll pay the rent; I'll pay the bill. 8
10. Goody, goody gumdrop, my son John! 9
11. Hot diggity dog! 9
12. How-ya' doin', ol' Scout? 10
13. Limit your worrin' to fifteen minutes a day. 10
14. Life is full of adjustments! 11
15. Thanks for the Memories; and Seventy-six Trombones. 12
16. It's in the other room. 13
17. Scoomy! . . . Scooby dooby! 13
18. Gitche Gumee. I'm gonna gitch your goomy! 14
19. Bless your heart; bless your bones; bless your Killarney-fied bones. . . 14

20. Gracious granny! (sigh — wheeee) O, Gracious granny, gracious granny! 15

21. Oh my lan! 16

22. My land O'Goshen! 16

23. Well I'm a redheaded Dutchman! 16

24. Nobody's said anything about my haircut. 17

25. I'm just tryin' to make a little conversation. 18

26. How 'bout that. 18

27. That's somebody's daughter. *or* That's somebody's son. 19

28. Come on! Let's go! It'll be dark in a minute! 19

29. The next house we build, we're gonna add a computer room. 20

30. Life's not too bad. It's really not. It's not bad at all. 21

31. Whadda ya' think o' that, you dirty rat? 22

32. Ah'right, ya' done it to my brudda', and now I'm gonna' do it to you! 23

33. It's a dirty trick! It sounds like a dirty trick to me! 24

34. Ya' ol' peench-head! 24

35. I'm not such a bad guy. In fact, I'm a pretty good guy once you get to know me! 25

36. I've had a lot of good training along the way. 25

37. Clean as you go. That's what I learned at the Toddle House. 26

38. Thank you very much. It's a pleasure doin' bidness wid-ja'! 27

39. Okay, kid; that's it — that's the size of it. 28

40. I sure do love ya'. You're not gonna' forget, are ya'? 28

41. I'm just tryin' to be of help. I'm not tryin' to hurt anybody — just tryin' to help ya' 'cause I love ya'. 29

42. Oh-loo-oook! 30

43. Hey-y-y, Pod-na-a-a! 30

44. Red-dio; pelly-kins; *and* herr-uh-c'n. 30

45. Ohhh...they're after ya'...they're gonna' gitche one way or the other. 31

46. Let's blow this firetrap. 32

47. Humburger! Humburger-roid! 32

48. Wun-a-ful! Wun-a-ful! 33
49. You're the best! Remember that, now. When you want to
    send the very best, send Margaret! 34
50. Hold-ja-tader. 35
51. I'm just a ham at heart! 35
52. I'm a patriot through and through! 36
53. I'm a cut-up at Rotary! 37
54. I'm a Tar Heel Fan! 38
55. I'm a Yankee fan…and was an Eagle fan! 40
56. I'm a golf fan and a Tiger Woods Fan! 41

PART TWO
Meaningful Thoughts

57. Thank you, Lord. Thank you, thank you, thank you! 45
58. Christianity is not a religion — it's a relationship. 45
59. Love is the greatest thing in the world. 46
60. You don't need legal advice — you need spiritual advice. . . . 47
61. When you're down and out, that's the very time you
    need to praise God and thank Him. 48
62. Adversity strengthens character. 49
63. Everything that happens to a Christian is filtered through
    God's fingers of love. 50
64. The Lord wants us to yield our lives and be willing to
    be led by Him. 50
65. A man of God in the will of God is immortal until
    his work on earth is done. 51
66. To see God's hand in everything makes life a great adventure. . 52
67. God's number one priority for His children is that we
    have an intimate relationship with Him. 53
68. Sufficient quality time with our heavenly Father is
    essential to having an intimate relationship with Him. 54

69. God's number one purpose for His children is that we
be conformed to the image and likeness of His Son. 54

70. If you were accused of being a Christian, would there be
enough evidence to convict you? 55

PART THREE

Favorite Bible Verses

71. "And you shall know the truth and the truth shall
make you free." John 8:32 59

72. "Jesus said to him, 'I am the way, the truth, and the life.
No one comes to the Father except through me.'" John 14:6 59

73. "All Scripture is given by inspiration of God, and is
profitable for doctrine, for reproof, for correction, for
instruction in righteousness." 2 Timothy 3:16 60

74. "For the time is coming when people will no longer listen
to sound doctrine and wholesome teaching. They will follow
their own desires and will look for teachers who will tell them
whatever their itching ears want to hear." 2 Timothy 4:3 (NLT) 61

75. "Beware lest anyone cheat you through philosophy and
empty deceit, according to the basic principles of the world
and not according to Christ." Colossians 2:8 62

76. "The grass withers, the flowers fade, but the Word of our
God stands forever." Isaiah 40:8 63

77. "The Word of God is living and powerful and sharper than
any two-edged sword, piercing even to the division of soul
and spirit, and of joints and marrow, and is a discerner of the
thoughts and intents of the heart." Hebrews 4:12 64

78. "For God so loved the world that He gave His only begotten
Son, that whoever believes in Him should not perish but
have everlasting life." John 3:16 64

79. "For by grace you have been saved through faith, and that
not of yourselves; it is the gift of God." Ephesians 2:8 65

80. "For He made Him who had no sin to be sin for us, that
we might become the righteousness of God in Him."
2 Corinthians 5:21 66

81. "Therefore, having been justified by faith, we have peace
with God through our Lord Jesus Christ." Romans 5:1 67

82. "For by one offering He has perfected those who are
being sanctified." Hebrews 10:14 68

83. "To them God willed to make known what are the
riches of the glory of this mystery among the gentiles:
which is Christ in you, the hope of glory." Colossians 1:27 68

84. "For as many as are led by the Spirit of God, these
are sons of God." Romans 8:14 69

85. "For if we live, we live to the Lord; and if we die, we
die to the Lord. Therefore, whether we live or die,
we are the Lord's." Romans 14:8 70

86. "Teach me Your ways, O Lord, that I may live according
to Your truth! Grant me purity of heart, so that I may
honor You." Psalms 86:11 (NLT) 71

87. "O God, You are my God; Early will I seek You; My
soul thirsts for You; My flesh longs for You in a dry and
thirsty land where there is no water." Psalms 63:1 72

88. "He who dwells in the secret place of the Most High shall
abide under the shadow of the Almighty." Psalms 91:1 72

89. "So then faith comes from hearing, and hearing by the
Word of God." Romans 10:17 73

90. "Therefore, if anyone is in Christ, he is a new creation;
old things have passed away; behold, all things have
become new." 2 Corinthians 5:17 74

91. "I have been crucified with Christ; it is no longer I who live,
but Christ lives in me; and the life I now live in the flesh
I live by faith in the Son of God who loved me and gave
Himself for me." Galatians 2:20 75

92. "For the message of the cross is foolishness to those who are perishing, but to us who are being saved it is the power of God." 1 Corinthians 1:18 76

93. "Don't you realize that your body is the temple of the Holy Spirit, who lives in you and was given to you by God? You do not belong to yourself." 1 Corinthians 6:19 (NLT). 76

94. "Do not be deceived, God is not mocked; for whatever a man sows, that he will also reap." Galatians 6:7 77

95. "For I am not ashamed of the gospel of Christ, for it is the power of God to salvation for everyone who believes, for the Jew first and also for the Greek." Romans 1:16 78

96. "For it is written: 'As I live, says the Lord, every knee shall bow to Me, and every tongue shall confess to God.'" Romans 14:11 . . . 79

97. "Trust in the Lord with all your heart, and lean not on your own understanding; in all your ways acknowledge Him, and He shall direct your paths." Proverbs 3:5-6 80

98. ". . . they received the Word with all readiness and searched the Scriptures daily to find out whether these things were so." Acts 17:11 81

99. "This is the day the Lord has made; we will rejoice and be glad in it." Psalm 118:24 81

100. "And whatever you do, do it heartily as to the Lord, and not to men." Colossians 3:23 82

101. "And we know that all things work together for good to those who love God, to those who are called according to His purpose." Romans 8:28 83

INTRODUCTION

In December of 2008, my wife Margaret had the bright idea of compiling a list of some of my favorite expressions so as to have a little fun on Christmas Day. Her idea was to share the list with the family as we gathered after our usual Christmas dinner at Aunt Carolyn's. Some expressions she considered comical, some kooky, and others just plain eccentric and original to me. She ended up with about twenty or twenty-five such expressions and we all had a good time laughing at my funny way of responding to various situations and events. Somebody commented that I ought to write a book about it.

I didn't think too much more about it until I was in the process of finalizing my third book, *My Greatest Discovery*, in order to send it to the publisher by August 1, 2009. That book was a rather serious account of my discovering the indwelling Holy Spirit, not only within myself, but also in each and every Christian. My second book, *The Game of Life . . . and How to Play It*, was also religious and serious in nature. Even the last two parts of my autobiography, *More then I Deserve*, were about my search for truth and spiritual growth as well as twenty-one lessons I learned along the way. One of the things I learned is to "Take life seriously, but not too seriously." In other words, we need to know who we are, how we are to live our lives, and where we are going, all in the context of our relationship with our Lord and Savior, Jesus Christ. But at the same time, we need to be able to put things in perspective. There are times when we need to lighten up. Laugh at life! Laugh at ourselves! Margaret has learned to do that quite well. She really enjoys laughing. Many times I've heard her in unrestrained belly laughter while she was all alone watching the antics of Hyacinth and Richard in *Keeping up Appearances*. Sometimes I'll be sitting with her, a smile on my face — maybe a slight undercurrent of inward amusement — while she is *rolling in the aisles*.

She'll say, "You don't think that's funny?" My nodding, smiling response will be something like, "Yeah, that *is* funny." She can even find a funny birthday card far more humorous than I can comprehend. I can see the funny part, but not necessarily with the deeper, hearty, uncontrolled, bring-you-to-tears laughter. Margaret reminds me from time to time of the therapeutic benefits of good, healthy laughter. She's right, as usual. I really made her day about a month ago when we were looking at a DVD of *The Odd Couple* with Walter Matthau and Jack Lemmon. There were at least three or four scenes where the odd couple more than lived up to their billing as being odd—they were hilariously odd, to put it mildly! I found myself out of control with a mixture of red-faced laughter and tears. I couldn't tell whether Margaret was as caught up in it as I was. All I know is that I was lost—in a different world—for as much as thirty or more seconds at a time.

Putting this Book in Perspective

So what is this book all about? Apparently, some of my responses that seem only natural to me, are perceived by some as being funny, odd, or even eccentric. I guess they are a part of my general makeup. Many outside my family may think I'm all seriousness, with no fun in my life. But they don't know all there is to know about the real me. In my three previous books, I've tried to be honest and realistic in my approach to each subject. Most of the time, the subject itself has required depth of understanding and a serious treatment. When you talk about heaven and hell and salvation and a relationship with Jesus Christ, there's little room for levity.

So this book is intended to show people my lighter side. My original objective was simply to list a number of the quirky expressions I use almost on a daily basis. Many of these are only known to Margaret and our three children, while some have been heard on the golf course, at the office, or among my closest friends. So I decided to accept the challenge issued by Margaret and the children, and "write a book about my crazy sayings."

Soon after I learned to read in the late 1930s, my mother and daddy gave me a book entitled *101 Famous Poems*. Not only did it have many of the popular traditional poems, but also there were a number of well-known prose documents, including the *Declaration of Independence,* the *Gettysburg Address,* and *The Ten Commandments*. I memorized some in their entirety, and others only the most familiar and often-quoted portions. By way of encouragement, Daddy paid me money to memorize them. For the longer poems such as Kipling's *If* and Longfellow's *The Day is Done,* Daddy gave me twenty-five cents. For the shorter ones such as *Trees* by Joyce Kilmer and *Crossing the Bar* by Alfred Tennyson, I got ten cents. That was back in the late 1930s and early 1940s, when the value of a dollar was quite different than it is today. The title of *101 Famous Poems* was an enticement to consider *101 Famous Sayings of Dan* for my title. Upon reflection, though, I realized there were only about thirty or thirty-five sayings original to me. Then I considered some thoughts of others that I have reflected on over the years. To expand my list to 101, I have also included some of my favorite Bible verses. So I have come up with 101 crazy sayings, meaningful thoughts, and favorite Bible verses that have been a part of my life for many years. I hope some will be considered light and funny, while others are more reflective and inspirational. In any event, they are destined to be a part of my legacy.

PART ONE

Some of My Crazy Sayings

1 ∽ **Great Caesar's Ghost! Great Jumpin' Jehosaphat!**

These two expressions are treated as one because, at least for me, one usually follows the other. I first saw them used in the Bat Man "funny books," as we used to call them back in my early childhood. I understand they are now referred to as "comic books." Back then, I don't remember saying either of these expressions out loud—just seeing them in print. It wasn't until I was in school at Woodberry Forrest that I first heard Jimmy Thompson exclaim with amazement, "Great Caesar's Ghost! Great Jumpin' Jehosaphat!" I don't recall why he said it, but it was his natural response to something unusual that we had seen, and it triggered my memory of Bat Man. I thought it was really cool, and I've been saying it ever since. Most of the time it just comes out when one of my children says something funny or when a golfing buddy makes a good shot.

2 ∽ **But I *like* burnt toast!**

That was a comment I made while visiting Frank Davenport at his home in Timmonsville, South Carolina. Frank and I were fraternity brothers in Kappa Sigma at UNC, and were also schoolmates at Woodberry Forest. Back about 1951, he invited several of his fraternity brothers for a weekend visit with his family. As we all gathered around the table to enjoy a good southern hospitality country breakfast of bacon, eggs, grits, sausage, ham, stewed apples and the works, it became obvious that something was wrong. Mrs. Davenport brought in a big plate of toast, some of which was quite dark. In fact, some of the pieces were "downright burnt." As the plate was passed to me, she apologized profusely. "Oh, I'm so sorry, Dan, let me get you another piece. You can't eat that!" In my feeble attempt to ease her embarrassment, I spouted out the immortal words, "But I *like* burnt toast!" I immediately picked up a piece and started eating it. There were a few muffled giggles, and even Mrs. Davenport replied, "No, no, no, Dan, you can't eat that. It's too burnt!" To which I replied, "But I *like* burnt toast! I really do!" I don't remember exactly how the episode ended, but I do remember I was determined to prove I not only could eat burnt toast, but I actually liked it. Even today, when I return from the table after answering the phone or speaking to a visitor at the door, I will say, "But I *like* soggy cereal" or "I *like* cold grits." Margaret and the children always get a kick out of that.

3   Don't worry about the mule goin' blind; you just load the cart!

I don't know where this originated, but it sounds like something Tyson Janny would have said at Woodberry. It's something I still say when Margaret or one of the children is concerned about doing a certain task and not trusting in the final outcome. Recently I asked Margaret about eating supper out on the patio. "But it looks like rain!" she said. My response was, "Don't worry about the mule going blind; you just load the cart." That may sound disrespectful, but she understood what I was saying and just laughed it off. This saying is a perfect response when someone is confronting a task and anxiously comments, "But 'what if' this...or 'what if' that." That is when it's appropriate to say, "Don't worry about the mule goin' blind; you just load the cart."

4   Let me show you a little trick I learned in the Roman Army many years ago.

I really don't know where I first heard my comment about the Roman Army. It could have been from George Bell, or maybe I just made it up. Maybe I'm trying to impress somebody about my vast background of information, or it could be I want my listener to know that I'm speaking with great authority and I know what I'm talking about. Why the Roman Army? I don't know. I use it a lot on the golf course when I'm about to bend a five iron shot around a tree and over the water to get on the green. Not everybody can make that shot—only those with extensive training acquired in the Roman Army. I've also used the Roman Army expression when I'm about to make a 45-foot, triple-breaking, downhill putt. After sighting it in and making my final approach to the ball, I'll say something like, "Now boys, I'm going to show you something I learned in the Roman Army many years ago. It's not really a hard putt if you know what you're doing." As you would guess, most of the time I miss, and the only comment my buddies make will be, "You didn't learn much did you?" But the one percent I do make, the crowd will say, "That's pretty good. How long ago were you in the Roman Army?" Just crazy chit-chatter!

5 ∾ Well I'll be jumped up and John dog my cats!

I heard this expression somewhere along the line many years ago, but it's been only in the past fifteen years or so that my golfing friend Charlie Brown has called it to my attention with pleasant frequency. While playing golf, he has come out with all kinds of crazy comments and odd sayings, but my favorite is, "Well I'll be jumped up and John dog my cats." He usually says it when explaining about a golf shot or responding to some comment made by Myron Hill or Kenneth Rouse to me. It comes so naturally with Charlie, and that's one reason I enjoy his company. For some reason, it has stuck with me and has even become part of my almost-daily vocabulary. It's so cute! "Well I'll be jumped up and John dog my cats!"

6 ∾ Do not worry, do not fret; just keep going without regret!

This little rhyming quip originated on the golf course when my partner Charlie Brown made a bad (or maybe I should say "less than good") golf shot. We had a tough match going, and Myron and Kenneth were about to whip us. It was critical that Charlie hit his second shot on number seventeen on the green. If we had a chance at all, he would have to put it on the green, close enough for a birdie if at all possible. Charlie usually came through pretty well when I needed him most, but this time I guess the pressure was too much for him. He popped it up and it landed in the middle of the pond. He knew I was counting on him, but when that ball plopped in the water, I calmly said, "Do not worry, do not fret; just keep going without regret!" That was my way of helping him see it wasn't the end of the world. "We've been beaten before, and we can handle the heartbreak again, if necessary." Ever since then, when any of us messes up, I'll say the same thing just to help us relax and not take our disappointment too seriously. I've made plenty of bad shots in my day, but Charlie always tries to make me feel good in spite of them. Of course, he doesn't have a standard answer like I do. I'll use this same rhyme at home if Margaret is worried about something I've done. Sometimes I say it right before another one of my quirky quips, "Do not worry, do not fret: just keep going without regret. Life is full of adjustments." (See #14.)

7 ❧ Sock-a-ma-roo-cha! Side-a-vays!

This is a golf expression coined by my buddy Carlton Oliver. Sometime in the mid 1970s, I was asked to join the foursome made up of Carlton, Ray Rouse, and Walker Sugg. Leslie Davis had been forced to drop out because of work commitments, and I was asked to take his place. One of the first things Carlton told me was that "we don't do any cussin' in this foursome. When we make a bad shot, the strongest language you can use is 'Sock-a-ma-roo-cha'" If it was a really bad shot, he added the phrase "Side-a-vays!" Both expressions were a figment of Carlton's rich imagination, and neither one makes any sense at all (at least to me). They are just made-up words — made to sound like you are really lambasting yourself for making such a stupid shot. Carlton did have one explanation for "Side-a-vays." He said it stood for "sideways." In other words, when you hit a ball way off line, you explain your emotion by exclaiming in loud disgust, "Sock-a-ma-roo-cha! Side-a-vays!" Every time I use those words, I think of my good buddy Carlton Oliver.

8 ～ Aan-ya-haash-a-me-ka! Naan-aan-taan-sha-nul! Sala-haam-ne-da! Wa-ta-koo-she-wa! Aana-tao-aai-she-ma-su! *and* Wa-tah-shi

This first "saying" is a bunch of gobbledygook words I learned from my Korean friend, Nam He Su, when I was in the Army in Korea. Nam He Su was a Republic of Korea (ROK) soldier who befriended me shortly after I arrived at Camp Casey, assigned to the 3rd Infantry Regiment of the 7th Armored Division. I asked him to teach me some Korean expressions so I could appear "fluent" when I got back home. The above words are what I remember. They are of my own phonetic spelling for ease of pronunciation. I still use them from time to time with family and friends just to show off and have a little fun. They were mostly used over the years on the golf course. When Carlton or I would make a bad shot or miss a short putt, it became routine for him to first say, "Sock-a-ma-roo-cha!" I would then add "Side-a-vays!" Then, to complete our routine as we walked off the green, I would start mumbling some of my Korean spiel to add to our show of disgust. I don't remember the actual meaning of any of the words, other than the familiar "hello", "goodbye", and "I love you."

Wa-tah-shi is entirely different. It's a Korean word that became part of the everyday vocabulary of all of us soldiers in Korea. The unofficial meaning of *Wa-tah-shi* is "me-the big guy-I'm in control" — that type of connotation. *Honcho* is another word with similar meaning, but is used in a different way. You might say, "Who's the *honcho* around here?" *Wa-tah-shi* is used by saying something like, "When you talk to Wa-tah-shi, you'd better listen, because he's somebody important."

I use it around the house in casual conversation with Margaret, such as when she tells me to be careful and not slip on the ice, or be sure to drive carefully. My standard response is, "Don't worry about Wa-tah-shi; I can take care of myself." This morning when I told her I would clean up the dishes, I said, "Just leave everything to Wa-tah-shi; I'll take care of it. Don't you worry about a thing." That was the least I could do after she prepared such a delicious

Saturday morning breakfast of ham and eggs, grits, and fried apples, along with the usual orange juice, milk, sliced oranges, toast, and banana bread. I may be *Wa-tah-shi* to her, but she's the Queen of the Dan Perry household to me.

9 ∽ Don't worry, I'll pay the rent; I'll pay the bill.

That certainly didn't originate with me, but I use it fairly often in instances such as when Margaret conservatively points out that maybe we don't need to stay at such an expensive motel. I guess I've reached the stage in life that I tend to want to go first class. Maybe we've pinched pennies long enough, so we can now reach for the gold and "enjoy life; it's later than you think." Anyway, I'm reminded of my daddy on the golf course. When I would have a long fairway wood to the green while players in front of us were still putting out, he would get a little anxious and want me to go ahead and shoot, thinking that I couldn't get there anyway. He would say, "Go ahead and shoot, I'll pay the bill." That brings to mind an occasion when I was playing golf with Frazier Bruton on the par-four number thirteen at Falling Creek Country Club. I pulled my drive in the rough leaving me about 185 yards to the green. The only problem was that I had a tree in front of me with low-hanging branches. To even come close to getting on the green I would have to aim way to the right and then draw the ball substantially to the left. I figured my 3-wood length was 185 yards at best, and to hit a draw shot that far would be out of the question. I waited a minute for the maintenance man to finish mowing the green, but he kept going. Then I decided to go ahead and shoot because I knew I had nothing to worry about. It would have to be a perfect shot to even come close. Well, would you believe I did hit a perfect shot? It barely missed the tree, curved around it beautifully and rolled right on the green in front of the maintenance man. I couldn't have hit that same shot again even if I tried a hundred times. Frazier had hit his drive in the right rough, so I drove the cart over to see him hit. While looking toward the green, we saw a cart moving toward us full speed ahead. In fact, he pulled up to us and said, "Did one of you hit that ball on the green while I was still mowing?"

He was obviously peeved. I knew I had done wrong and apologized profusely as he scolded me for my lack of golf etiquette. The good news is I didn't have to "pay the rent": and Daddy didn't have to "pay the bill" posthumously.

10 ⤳ Goody, goody gumdrop, my son John!

This is an oldie I remember from childhood. Maybe it was just "Goody, goody gumdrop" when something good happened. I don't remember how I came to add "my son John" to the ending. Maybe it was from Charlie Brown. At any rate, it took our one and only grandchild to jog my memory. Our baby girl Radford and her husband Chad are the proud parents of Virginia Carolyn Pharr, who, at this writing, has just turned five years old. She is named after Chad's grandmother, Virginia Pharr, and Margaret's sister, Carolyn Hodges. Virginia is at the perfect age to get excited about anything good. When her face lights up upon hearing we're taking her swimming, for example, I join the celebration with my "Goody, goody gumdrop, my son John," and off we go happily to the pool.

11 ⤳ Hot diggity dog!

This is quite a bit more special than just "Hot dog!" Sometimes it comes on the heels of "Hot dog," so the best expression is "Hot dog! Hot diggity dog!" To make it really special, I'll start off with "Goody, goody gumdrop, my son John!" and then move right into "Hot dog! Hot diggity dog!" and then come back with a final "Goody, goody gumdrop, my son John!" When you put 'em all together, they set the stage for a really high-pitched, exciting time. I catch myself quite regularly expressing the full routine when Virginia is around. She's at the perfect age to be the target of my silly antics and juvenile behavior. The more excited she gets, the more excited I get. I enjoy egging her on as she innocently responds to her Gran Dan, totally innocent and unaware of how she is being set up to carry on with such frivolity. When Virginia's around, it's so easy for me to say, "Hot diggity dog!"

12   How-ya' doin', ol' Scout?

It was "way back when" that my brother Ely, Jr., introduced me to the expression, "Ol' Scout." I didn't think too much about it the first few times he said it, but after a while it became his custom to greet certain friends with, "How-ya' doin', ol' Scout?" I think it probably started when he was in med school at Carolina. I would go see him in his dorm room just to see how things were going. After opening the door, he would greet me, "How-ya' doin', ol' Scout?" Somehow or other, the phrase just grew on me and I got in the habit of using it, but to a much less degree than Ely. Actually, it lay dormant in my memory for some forty years. Then, about ten years ago, I realized I was using that long-lost phrase, "How-ya' doin', ol' Scout?" or "Good work, ol' Scout," or "Way to go, ol' Scout!" One night before our Bible study began, Ford Coley and I were in casual conversation when he paid me an unusual compliment, saying, "Dan, I like the way you say Old Scout. That's really neat." And he repeated himself: "Old Scout — I like that." I never thought about it as being a neat thing to say, for it was (and still is) a natural part of my everyday vocabulary.

13   Limit your worrin' to fifteen minutes a day.

Let me give you a follow-up story to the first time I remember hearing the term, "Ol' Scout" back when Ely was in med school at Carolina. One day he and his roommate, Frank Stallings, were seated at their desks, apparently studying, when Ely greeted me with the usual ol' Scout routine. I responded by saying, "I'm fine, how're ya'll? Whatcha'll doin'?" Then came the most unusual answer I had ever heard. Still seated at his desk, Frank said, "We're worrin'." "Whatcha mean, worrin'?" I replied quite puzzled. "Well," Frank said, "we've got a lot going on in med school, a lot of homework, and late hours that cause us a lot of concern. Frankly, we're really worried, but we decided we can't spend all our time worrin', so the best thing to do is to set aside fifteen minutes each day to do nothing but worry. By limiting our worry time to fifteen minutes, we can spend the rest of the day studying and getting something done. So that is what we were doing when you came in — we were doing some heavy worrin'. Our fifteen minutes is about up, so now we can enjoy the rest of the day." All three of us had a good laugh! If you think about it, it makes right good sense. We don't need to spend all our time worrying. In fact, the Bible tells us to, "Be anxious for nothing . . ." (Philippians 4:6). Until we can learn to abide by that truth, the best thing is to consciously limit our worrying to fifteen minutes, or less, a day. I tell that story from time to time to try to help a troubled friend see the futility of spending any time worrying. I've found it doesn't help a bad situation get better. It only serves to hurt our general well-being. When Paul advises us to *be anxious for nothing*, he follows with the next phrase, ". . . but in everything by prayer and supplication, with thanksgiving, let your requests be made known to God; and the peace of God, which surpasses all understanding will guard your hearts and minds through Christ Jesus." What he's saying is that we should put our dependency on God and His peace, rather than relying on our own limited wisdom and understanding.

14 ∽ Life is full of adjustments!

We all know there's quite a bit of truth in this statement. We have to make adjustments in things we wear, in things we use, and life in general. Some adjustments are minor and some are major, but in either case they are adjustments. I find myself saying this to Margaret quite frequently, in relation to insignificant things, as a way of encouragement and good humor. So whenever things don't go exactly according to plans, that's when I'll move on by saying, "Life is full of adjustments — we'll just have to change plans!" I say that for the benefit of both of us as a reminder that sometimes one's best-laid plans simply don't work out for one reason or another. I often say it halfway in jest, not only to Margaret, but also to myself, such as when I spill something on my tie and have to change as we rush out the door to church or a dinner engagement, or when Radford calls from Asheville saying she and Virginia will be a day late in coming to Kinston because Chad needs her to work at their *Pineapple Jack's* restaurant a little longer than first expected. In such times, the only thing we can do is adjust to the change of circumstances, for Life is indeed "full of adjustments." Other, more serious, adjustments had to be made after Margaret broke her leg in June of 2008, and I tore my rotator cuff the following September. Although she's now walking without a cane, she still has stiffness and lingering pain and can't get around like she once could. I haven't been able to play golf in more than a year and a half; and if I ever do play again, it will be on a limited basis. I won't be able to hit the ball like I once could. Of course, I realize old age has something to do with it. Adjusting our lives to the passing of years requires us all to realize, "Life in full of adjustments." There's nothing we can do about it, so why not find a way to laugh at it and have a little fun while making those inevitable adjustments.

15 ∽ Thanks for the Memories; and Seventy-six Trombones.

Comedian Bob Hope's closing theme song was *Thanks for the Memories*, and as he sang each stanza, he would always list several memories that rhymed, and then conclude with "... thank you so much." That was during the era of Jack Benny, Fibber McGee and Molly, and Edgar Bergen and Charlie McCarthy in the 1930s, '40s and '50s. When my children were growing up in the 1970s and '80s, somehow I got on a jig singing Bob Hope's theme song, except instead of *Thanks for the Mem'ries*... I would improvise. Thank you *for the mem-o-ries*, and continue with "... *of sunny afternoons, of big, fat baboons, and little skinny raccoons — oh, thank you so much.* The children thought I was a little wacky singing about big, fat baboons and little, skinny raccoons. The fact that it didn't make any sense made it all the funnier to Elizabeth, Daniel, and Radford. They used to kid me about how, all of a sudden, I would break out into *Oh-h-h, thank you for the mem-o-ry* . . . . I still sing it (for no reason at all), and they still think I'm a silly old Daddy. I've also been known to start singing out of the clear blue the theme song to the *The Music Man*. Sometime I'll prance around with the Robert Preston strut and sing *Seventy-six trombones led the big parade, with a hundred-and-ten cornets close at hand.* It's a snappy marching tune that comes to the surface of my mind out of nowhere. When it does, I can't help but march and strut with Professor Harold Hill as I sing. Sometimes I'll just whistle or hum it. Either way, it's still a lot of fun and my children still think I'm crazy.

16 ⤚ **It's in the other room.**

Margaret and our children kid me all the time about certain peculiar sayings I come up with. When they ask me where a book is or where Margaret's coat is, instead of identifying the specific room, I just give a standard answer, "It's in the other room." The way I say it, it may be in the bedroom, or the dining room, or the den. They always laugh when I talk about "the other room." That means little or nothing to anyone else, except to Margaret and the children, it's just another one of Daddy's crazy sayings that provokes a laugh and a comment every time. It looks like I'm the only one who knows which room I'm talking about —and sometimes I don't even know. Perhaps I don't have any idea where Margaret's glasses are and I'm just trying to make conversation. It also could be that I'm unconsciously telling them, "I don't have your glasses. You need to look somewhere else." Whatever the reason, it's just another one of my quirky expressions.

17 ⤚ **Scoomy!... Scooby dooby!**

This is one of those expressions that even amazes me. I'm sure the reader has no earthly idea what it means, or how it originated. So here's how it got started and how it evolved into one of my crazy, quirky expressions: At certain times of the year I, like many of you, have allergic reactions resulting in episodes of sneezing or coughing or clearing the throat. I could always tell when Daddy or brother Warren was in an audience or crowd by the way they cleared their throats. Even yesterday, while we were attending Bogue Banks Baptist Church at the beach, Margaret said she knew Barbara was there because she heard her sneeze. Lo and behold, she was right. As the service ended and we were filing out, there Barbara was. I had seen Betty Blaine and Ashley, but had no idea Barbara was there. My mother taught me to say "Excuse me" after I sneezed or coughed. I guess I said it so much that I shortened *excuse me* by leaving off the *ex*, resulting in *'scuse me*; then it was shortened to *scoomy*. Being the ham that I am, it was only natural to add the words, *scooby dooby*. It somehow makes sense to me, even though I'm sure most folks think it's another foreign language

13

thrown in just like all those meaningless Korean expressions I use from time to time. At least I try to remember my manners by saying "excuse me," even though it may be in a foreign language known only to me.

18 ～ Gitche Gumee. I'm gonna gitch your goomy!

Crazy! Crazy! Crazy! It even sounds crazy to me, and I'm sure it sounds even crazier to you. In my *101 Famous Poems* book, Longfellow's *Hiawatha's Child-hood* appears on page 25. I have always been fascinated with the opening words: "By the shores of Gitche Gumee, by the shinning Big-Sea-Water, stood the wigwam of Nokomis, daughter of the Moon Nokomis . . . ." We studied at least portions of the famous poem at Woodberry. The name Gitche Gumee (pronounced Goomy) has always attracted my attention. It stands out like a spot light in a dark room. I sometimes use the words Gitche Gumme when responding to something Margaret has or hasn't done. Sometimes for no reason at all, I'll just say *Gitche-Gumee.* And most of the time I will follow with the inevitable words, *I'm gonna get your goomy.* It doesn't mean a thing It just comes out. Sometimes it's a natural follow up to *Scoomy* when I sneeze or cough, because it rhymes. Margaret reminded me that I sometimes say, *They're gonna gitch your goomy!* Just a little light-hearted foolishness.

19 ～ Bless your heart; bless your bones; bless your Killarney-fied bones.

Many of us from time to time will say, "Bless your heart," to express our approval as a "thank you" for some favor or kind deed. I love the way my sister-in-law, Carolyn Hodges, says it rather pitifully with her southern drawl: "Bless your hoart." Her pronunciation of the word "heart" makes it special. Ralph Shell, long-time Kinston podiatrist of years ago, used to say "bless your heart" quite frequently and with sincere affection. It's such a tender phrase, not only when spoken softly but also as an exclamation: "Well, bless your heart!" I've been saying it most all my life, but I guess it must have been in the 1970s that I converted it to "Bless your bones." Our long-time, good Christian friend, Dotty Carter, apparently loves the way I say "Bless your bones" when I greet her after a long absence. In fact, often she will say it before I do. But what about "Killarney-fied bones? According to the *World Book Encyclopedia*, Killarney is a small town in southern Ireland. It is mentioned in at least one Irish ballad that is quite appealing to me when sung by an Irish tenor. There's something about the name Killarney that rings a bell with me. When I think of Killarney, I think of the green meadowlands and quaint villages of that beautiful little country, Ireland. How I came to add it to "bless your bones," I'll never know, other than the fact they just seem to flow together. "Bless your bones; bless your Killarney-fied bones." Like most of my expressions, it has meaning only for me. Put all three phrases together and you have a strange but sincere expression: *Bless your heart; bless your bones; bless your Killarney-fied bones.*

20 ⁓ **Gracious granny! (sigh — wheeee) O, Gracious granny, gracious granny!**

Whenever we get frustrated over a situation, or if we are just plain tired at the end of a long day, we all tend to let off steam by making some comment to show our feelings. I guess we all have some favorite expression we use for that purpose. Betty Blaine said hers is "Land O' Goshen!" Her mother Barbara's favorite expression in such situations is "Dear Gussy!" Mine seems to be "Gracious granny!" Depending on the nature and/or severity of the circumstances, I may add one or two other gracious grannies for emphasis. Many times when I say "gracious granny," I think of my good friend, Suzanne Wooten. Her two cute grandchildren, Olivia and Carrington, each call her "Granny." Her husband Sonny also calls her "Granny" from time to time. Although I seldom use the name in referring to Suzanne, I do think of her quite frequently when I say "gracious granny." Most of the time I will follow with a slight sigh or "wheee" before following up with a couple of repeats, ". . . Oh, gracious granny, gracious granny." Oddly enough, I don't necessarily have to be tired when I say it. Sometimes I use it to express amazement at a situation. Sometimes, when getting up in the morning and feeling stiff in my joints, I'll mumble in a low but expressive voice, "Gracious granny...." Other times I say it with a little sigh just to be talking and saying something.

21 ❧ Oh my lan!

This was one of my mother's frequently-used expressions. Whenever she was surprised at an unusual situation or caught off guard by some uncommon happening, her response was usually "Oh my land!" But she didn't pronounce the "d" in "land." It was a brisk "Oh my lan!", all in one quick breath. Soon after Mother died in 1983, I began saying "Oh my lan" in remembrance of her, and have been saying it ever since. Although I use it automatically, many times for no reason at all, I still retain an image of Mother and the way she used to say *Oh my lan!*

22 ❧ My land O'Goshen!

Biblical scholars will remember that the land of Goshen was the area of the Nile River delta where Jacob and his family settled under the protection of their brother, Joseph, Egypt's prime minister at the time. As mentioned in #20 above, Betty Blaine says "Land of Goshen" when she's tired or frustrated over something. I say it under the same conditions, but also when exclaiming over being surprised at an unusual circumstance. It seems to fall in line with *Great Caesar's Ghost! Great Jumpin' Jehosaphat! My land O' Goshen!* Also it's not uncommon for me to first say, "O my Lan" and then pause a second or two and say, 'My land O' Goshen!"

23 ❧ Well I'm a redheaded Dutchman!

As far as I know, this saying originated with my father. I heard him say it numerous times, mostly when he got excited upon hearing some good news. On Christmas Day, 1962, I had heard him say it with more enthusiasm than ever before. I had asked Margaret to marry me on Christmas Eve night. After the midnight service at the First Presbyterian Church, we drove down Queen Street to Gordon Street Christian Church where I had prearranged with our youth minister, Tommy Norvell, to have a key to the sanctuary. It was there in the beauty of that setting that we became engaged to be married. The next day, I got the necessary permissions from her mother. Now it was time to tell my mother and daddy. We drove to my home place at 908 West Road where Mother and Daddy were seated at the card table playing their customary game of gin rummy. They were calm and easy, concentrating on the next card play. But when we broke the news, I've never seen Daddy so excited! He jumped up from his seat, pranced across the room in front of the fireplace and exclaimed, "Well I'm a redheaded Dutchman!" I think he may have said it more that once, each time with more gusto! I can hear him now as he gave Margaret and me his resounding approval: "Well I'm a redheaded Dutchman!" Since that time, I have occasionally used those same words as a memorial to Daddy and that unforgettable Christmas Day. I might add that the way he said it, there was no time for any punctuation after the "Well." He just let it roll right out; *Well I'm a redheaded Dutchman*!

24 ∾ Nobody's said anything about my haircut.

This was another of my father's pet comments. I remember on numerous occasions he would come in the house after getting a new haircut, and greet Mother with the usually welcome kiss. One of the first things he would say was, "Nobody's said anything about my haircut." Oftentimes he would say it before she even had time to take notice. That was just his way of letting it be known, with somewhat of a bragging overtone, that something was different about him. "Just look, I've had a haircut and nobody's even noticed it!" That was also another way of his having a little fun in expressing his love and devotion for the lady of his life. Today I use those same words with an additional phrase at the beginning. At the end of the day, after I've been home for a while where I can be seen by Margaret, I'll sometimes say, "I've been here all day long and nobody's said anything about my haircut." As with Daddy, I'm just poking a little fun at dear Margaret.

25   I'm just tryin' to make a little conversation.

Often I'll tack on to the end of "Nobody's said anything about my haircut," and other such silly phrases, the little statement, "I'm just tryin' to make a little conversation." I guess that's my way of offering some rationale for the haircut comment. It's all a part of having a little meaningless fun. Margaret understands exactly what I mean as I carry on. She often gives a little snicker as a casual sign of approval as well as forgiveness for my nonsensical behavior. The other day, when I told her I was writing about some of those things, she made an interesting comment. She said, "You're not going to be able to get much reaction from your readers, because it's not so much what you say, but how you say it. You can't convey the facial expressions and tone of voice with pen and paper." I guess she had a point. But, for better or worse, I am who I am, and whatever I say, it's just a natural response from a "ham at heart" and silly ol' me at that.

26   How 'bout that.

Son Daniel is always noticing the way I say, "How 'bout that." I don't even realize I'm saying it until he repeats after I say it — just a reminder that, *There, I've said it again.* It usually comes out after Margaret or one of the children tell an interesting story or some interesting fact. But it's not unusual for me to say, "How 'bout that" at the conclusion of a television program or after some comment made on the radio. Most of the time it's soft-spoken, with no excitement or animation — just a gentle, almost under my breath, "How 'bout that." That's when Daniel follows with the same soft, almost inaudible, "How 'bout that." You notice it's not punctuated with either a question mark or exclamation point. The reason is simple: even though it's in the form of a question, it's not spoken as a question. Neither is it in the form of an exclamation. I'm not shouting out "How about that!" No, it's just a quiet, soft-spoken comment, "How 'bout that."

27 〜 That's somebody's daughter. *or* That's somebody's son.

Even the toughest of us and those who seem insensitive to the needs of others have a soft spot in our hearts under certain conditions. From time to time, we've all seen a scraggly young teen-aged girl with a backpack trudging along a highway — going somewhere, anywhere. My first thought is *That poor girl must be running away from home. I'm sure her parents have no idea she's out there just waiting to be picked up by a strange man, an opportunist hoping for excitement.* That's the kind of pitiful sight that causes me to think to myself, and say out loud if Margaret is with me, "That's somebody's daughter." We've also seen a ragged-looking, bearded man standing at a busy intersection at the beach holding a homemade sign advertising his plight, *Will work for food — I need a job!* Then is when I'll say, "That's somebody's son." I can't help but think of the mother and /or daddy and the home environment in which those children were reared. *Why is that man hungry and penniless?* Even though that standard response is sincerely spoken, there are times when Daniel has kidded me in a much lighter vein when we see a boy or girl just innocently walking along. He'll beat me to the punch by saying, "That's somebody's daughter" or "That's somebody's son."

28 〜 Come on! Let's go! It'll be dark in a minute!

I first heard Mr. J.W. Montgomery say this while at the Kinston Country Club during the early 1940s. Ever since I was old enough to play golf, we had a family foursome with Daddy and my brothers, Warren and Ely, Jr. We played whenever we could all get together, but most Saturday afternoons, Daddy continued with his old foursome of J.W. "Slim" Montgomery, Tom Harvey Sr. and Julian "Snide" McCullen. Others who joined them from time to were British Long, E.R. "Buck" Wooten, A.H. "Bootsy" Jeffress and G.A. Bowles. That was quite a crew! Each was a character in his own right, with unique little quirks and silly sayings. When I was old enough to carry Daddy's bag, I would caddy for him, and always looked forward to the fun and camaraderie they had together. On one particular day we were a few minutes late, which was unusual for Daddy, for he always stressed punctuality. As Daddy and I were emerging from the "caddy house," Ol' Slim yelled out, "Come on, Ely! Let's go! It'll be dark in a minute!" Slim, along with Snide and Tom, were waiting on the first tee and it was two minutes after one o'clock on a beautiful sunshiney day. They were waiting and raring to go! As we hurriedly approached the tee box, Slim reminded Daddy once more, "Don't you know it's late? It'll be dark in a minute!" Slim's son, John, lives in Charlotte and occasionally comes to Kinston or the beach. Each time we get together, I remind him of that memorable summer day over sixty-five years ago when his daddy yelled out in his own inimitable way, "Come on Ely! Let's go! It'll be dark in a minute!" Sometimes I'll say the same thing to Margaret or one of the children when waiting to go somewhere. Who else but Slim Montgomery could come up with the words, "It'll be dark in a minute" in the middle of a beautiful, sunny, summer's day?

Postscript: When I was at home writing about this incident, I asked Margaret how to spell "camaraderie" and then later "inimitable." It turned out, I had to look up both words in my dictionary. As she was leaving the house a few minutes later she said, "Why do you have to use such hard-to-spell words?" My answer was, "Because those are the best words I can think of to describe those particular situations." And that's the way it is.

29 ⮞ **The next house we build, we're gonna add a computer room.**

Margaret often reminds me that I ought to be using my personal computer more. Daniel uses it to check his E-mail every time he comes to see us, which is at least three or four times a week. Radford, who lives in Ashville, uses it when she comes for a visit, which is generally two or three times a year. And I hardly ever use it. I find it can be very time-consuming to go to the trouble to put it in place on my desk, open it up, turn it on—and then turn it off, close it up and put it in its proper place. A lot of people spend way too much time on their computers. They can even get addicted to them. As much fun and informative as it can be, I find I would rather spend my spare time reading, writing, and studying. I just don't have it in my routine to use a computer on a daily basis, sending and answering E-mails, etc. I might feel differently if it remained permanently open and set up along with a printer at a separate desk or in a different room. It's just too much trouble otherwise. When Margaret comments about my not using my computer, I kid her back by responding, "The next time we build a house, we'll add a computer room." We both know full well we've already built our last house and this is it! Similarly with my ten-by-twelve-foot home study, this should be plenty big for my little mess plus some of hers. We have one floor-to-ceiling bookcase plus three half-shelves. We thought that would give us plenty of room for my books. The problem is I didn't know I would be collecting so many. I get books on a monthly basis from David Jeremiah and Charles Stanley plus I'm always ordering other books of interest. Space has run out. They're stacked in the chair, on the floor, everywhere! I kid Margaret about it by saying, "The next time we build a house, we'll build a separate room, a special library, just to take care of my books." Even though she's heard that story before, she manages to giggle a little as she rolls her eyes in mild disgust.

Postscript: Several weeks after writing about the burden of moving, setting up, and taking down my laptop, we asked our expert friend Don Lingg to come around and give us some advice about updating our system. One of his suggestions was to clear off the nearby table originally set aside for Margaret's painting paraphernalia. I don't know why we didn't think of that long before now, because it's made my PC more readily available, at least for Daniel. I still hardly ever use it.

30 ∽ Life's not too bad. It's really not. It's not bad at all.

This is a comment I make to Margaret when she gets down and complains about something that's frustrating her. Yesterday she was worn out with grocery shopping, mainly because she couldn't find several items on her list. By way of offering a sympathetic ear and at the same time adding a little lighthearted sarcastic tone to my voice, I said my usual, "Life's not too bad. It's really not. It's not bad at all." I find that saying this sometimes helps. In any event, it's just a comment I make from time to time. I may say it as we admire the beautiful setting of our backyard patio with the flowing fountain against the backdrop of the brick and stucco wall surrounded by the flowering confederate jasmine. Potted red dipladenias are spotted around on the miniature monkey grass with larger potted blue plumbagos at the corner of the patio itself. In the midst of praising the Lord and thanking Him for our many blessings, sometimes I say, "Life's not too bad, is it?" Many years ago, I heard my friend Sonny Wooten say, as he heartily approved of a delicious steak, "That ain't half bad." Sometimes, for emphasis, I'll tack Sonny's expression onto the end of my own: "Life's not too bad—it ain't half bad." When I do, I always think of Sonny Wooten. I guess counting our blessings with a little sarcasm is alright at times, but nothing takes the place of a sincere, "Thank you, Lord, for being so good to us. I'm so grateful for your grace and mercy."

31 ⟶ Whadda ya' think o' that, you dirty rat?

"Take that, you dirty rat," is one of the famous lines of James (Jimmy) Cagney. Everybody knows that—in fact, I think I actually heard him say it many, many years ago in one of his gangster movies. I could hardly believe my ears when I saw a video replay of the special Hollywood Lifetime Achievement Award given to Cagney shortly before he died. Among his responding comments he said, "And by the way, I never said, 'Take that, you dirty rat!'" I really think he was kidding, because I'm almost sure I heard him say it. Whether he said it or not, it's certainly attributable to him, and I catch myself jokingly saying it quite often. Just this morning, as we were in Greensboro staying at the O. Henry Hotel, after finishing our prayer time, I said, "Alright now, let me feed you a good breakfast. What do you think o' that, you dirty rat?" Margaret and I had driven Bumpsie LaRoque and Molly Smith to Greensboro on July 11, 2009, to attend the 50th anniversary celebration of Mary and John Broome. It was a wonderful occasion which afforded family and friends the opportunity not only to "roast" this fine couple, but also to share some meaningful comments in appreciation for their fifty years of married life. By the way, I don't usually call Margaret a "dirty rat" in public because she's just the opposite—she's a sweet, dear thing. It's just that, at certain times, somewhere along the way, the occasion just calls for a "dirty rat" comment. It just comes out naturally, "Whadda ya' think o' that, you dirty rat?"

For a little variety, I might say, "How about that, you dirty rat!" I tend to use them interchangeably. It's important, though, not to confuse this with #26: "How 'bout that," which is simple and softspoken, said almost under my breath. #31 is used more emphatically, with much more feeling and animation. "How about that, you dirty rat" emphasizes *a-bout* with two syllables and *that* and *rat* as rhyming. Each expression is used in different circumstances, but each is part of my everyday vocabulary.

32 ∿ Ah'right, ya' done it to my brudda', and now I'm gonna' do it to you!

This is also one of those James Cagney lines that just sorta' sticks with me. I never know when I'm going to say it. Of course, the sequence of events is Cagney's brother had been murdered by the "dirty rat" standing right there in Cagney's presence. Now it was Cagney's chance to get even. I can see him now, with his teeth clinched in his scrunched-up little mouth, pistol in hand, and ready to carry out his get-even threat, "Ah' right, ya' done it to my brudda', and now I'm gonna' do it to you!" Bang! Bang! Bang! "Take that, you dirty rat!" I don't watch gangster movies any more. For some reason, they just don't appeal to me, but that scene has lingered in my mind for over sixty years. I hope none of you takes offense if I happen to use my "dirty rat" routine in your presence. It's just a part of my warped personality. Of course, to make it really effective, you've got to give it that James Cagney personal touch. You've got to say it softly, but with feeling— almost in a whisper. In other words, you've gotta' be cool as a cucumber but mean as a snake. Then you've gotta' be prepared to follow through with a bang! Bang! Bang! "Take that, you dirty rat!"

33 ⤳ It's a dirty trick! It sounds like a dirty trick to me!

Many years ago, I heard a lady say, in a rather serious tone, "It's a dirty trick," Through no fault of her own, she was frustrated and even distraught at her unfortunate situation. In a saddened voice she simply said, "It's a dirty trick."

Although this phrase was born out of difficult conditions, I have come to use it in a much lighter vein, under totally different circumstances. Whenever Margaret or I experience some mild disappointment, when something doesn't go quite right, I'll say in a kidding manner, "It's a dirty trick." When a rainy day spoils our plans to go to the beach, or Margaret is frustrated when she misplaces a book or her reading glasses, I'll often say with tongue in cheek, "It's a dirty trick—sounds like a dirty trick to me!" Most of the time, Margaret will respond, "It *is* a dirty trick!" That's her lighthearted way of going along with my fun and sarcasm.

34 ⤳ Ya' ol' peench-head!

As far as I know, this originated with Frank Stallings, brother Ely's room-mate when they were in medical school at Carolina. They were in the class of 1954, which was the first four-year UNC med school class, so I think it was about 1952 when I heard Frank say it. I think it's probably spelled p-i-n-c-h head, but the pronunciation is like p-e-e-n-c-h head, which means the "i" is pronounced like the "i" in *ink*. The word "peench-head" can be used any time there's a little bit of frustration involved. One of the first times I remember using the word "peench-head," somebody asked me where in the world I got the word "pinch-head." I said, "No, it not pinch-head, it's "peench-head." I used to use it a lot on the golf course after missing a short putt. I'd take out my dismay and frustration on the ball and cry out, "Ya' ol' peench-head." I'm fully aware that it wasn't the ball's fault. I'm the one who missed the putt. The ball merely went where I putted it, but that didn't keep me from talking bad about that sorry golf ball, "Ya' ol' peench-head!" Often when Carlton Oliver would make a bad shot and say "sock-a-ma-roo-cha!" I would register my agreement by adding "ya' ol' peench-head!" That was also a good time for me to follow with some of my Korean nonsense words. It was all in fun — just our way of adding a little spice to the game.

35 ∼ I'm not such a bad guy. In fact, I'm a pretty good guy once you get to know me!

This may seem like I'm bragging on myself, and telling the world what a great guy I am, but that's not it at all. Occasionally, I may say this to one of the children or maybe even to Margaret's sister, Carolyn, when she comes for supper on Monday nights. But most of the time I say it to Margaret after I've done her an unexpected favor or been a good boy in the kitchen. When she goes to the kitchen and discovers I've already cleaned up, she'll thank me for being so considerate and helpful. Then is when I'll say in a serious but lighthearted way, "You're certainly welcome. Ya' know, I'm not such a bad guy. In fact, I'm a pretty good guy once you get to know me." She'll usually respond by saying, "Yeah, you're a pretty good guy. In fact you're a real good guy." Another thing I say quite often is, "I'm a good fellow when I sleep. I just don't sleep enough." I got that from brother Ely when we were growing up. He used to kid me by saying, "Dan, you're a pretty good boy (pause) when you sleep (pause). You just don't sleep enough." This type of exchange is just another one of the ways we tell each other "I love you."

36 ∼ I've had a lot of good training along the way.

This line usually follows the "I'm not such a bad guy line" mentioned above, although not necessarily. Often it's just my natural response when Margaret or a dinner guest pays me a compliment for cleaning up or doing some unexpected chore. What I'm really doing is paying Margaret a compliment by recognizing the expert training she has given me during our more than forty-seven years of married life. I'm saying to Margaret, "Thanks for the compliment, but the truth is I owe it all to you for training me so well."

When one of the children says something that warrants such a response, I'll tell them about how my mother and daddy taught Warren, Ely, and me to help out by washing the dishes and cleaning up the kitchen. This was not only good training for us three boys, but it also was a help to Mother. We started out with brother Warren doing the heavy work. This was in the 1930s, long before we got our first dishwasher—so he washed the dishes. Ely, Jr. was two years younger, so he did the drying and helped train his baby brother who was five years his junior. I was only four or five when I went into training. I first put up the knives, forks, and spoons. After I was old enough to be trusted with the dishes, I would put them in the cabinet. When Warren went off to Woodberry, I graduated to be the chief dryer and, when Ely left, I had the whole responsibility to myself. Mother taught me how to set the table, with knives, pointed out, spoons on the right, and forks and napkins on the left. She also taught me to say "Thank you for my good meal" or "I enjoyed my breakfast." To this day, I always (or nearly always) say, "I enjoyed my dinner" (or whatever). Many times after taking the dishes off the table and heading to "the other room," it'll all of a sudden come to me and I'll holler back to Margaret, "I enjoyed my supper!"

37 ∽ Clean as you go. That's what I learned at the Toddle House.

Back in the 1950s, there was a small "hole in the wall" quick-order restaurant called the Toddle House. Located across from Saint Mary's College in Raleigh, it was a popular place for young people to frequent for a cheeseburger, a Sunday morning breakfast, or a midnight snack. Bacon and eggs and grits, pancakes, and waffles were always good, especially late at night. A bunch of us boys would go by the Toddle House for a midnight snack after taking our dates back to Saint Mary's. We would always be hungry when we ate at the Toddle House. All it consisted of was a long counter with ten or twelve barstools. As far as I recall there were no booths—just stools in front of the counter. While the food itself was great, what went on behind the counter was something to behold! Most of the time there was only one man (occasionally two during the rush hour). It was fascinating to see him work with his white apron neatly around him (I don't remember a baker's hat). He took our orders without pencil and pad, and then turned around to begin his magic show. He would be cooking five, six, and seven things all at the same time. We all enjoyed observing his discipline and efficiency as he flipped the pancakes in the skillet, checked the waffles, turned the hamburgers and sausage, drained the crackling bacon, popped up the toast, and watched the stewed apples all at the same time. In between chores, he would go to the refrigerator, pour the orange juice, and give us our milk or coffee. He was an expert at what he did—poetry in motion. And to top it all, while at the stove he would have a spatula in one hand and a cleaning rag in the other. Every time he made a mess or saw a crumb in his kitchen, it was gone in no time. His motto was "Clean as you go," and he did just that. In all the times I went there, his kitchen was spotless. I never saw a mess. This cook was the envy of us all. In fact, while most little boys wanted to be a fireman or garbage collector so they could ride the truck, all of us boys wanted to be a Toddle House cook. Even today when I make a mess on the kitchen counter, I'll sometimes (not all the time, but sometimes) grab a rag and immediately clean it up—and say with fond memory of the good ol' days, "Clean as you go! That's what I learned at the Toddle House!"

38 ∽ Thank you very much. It's a pleasure doin' bidness wid-ja'!

When I say, "Thank you very much," I'm often reminded of my golfing buddy Charlie Brown (not to be confused with the comic strip character). When Charlie makes a long putt, he usually says, "Thank you very much." Just reading those written words does not do justice to the way Charlie says it. He uses a noticeably profound slur as he mumbles almost under his breath. It comes out something like "Thank ya' v'ry muuch"—just like Elvis Presley. Can't you just see ol' Elvis responding to the screaming crowd—feebly trying to calm them down? "Thank ya' v'ry muuch—thank ya' v'ry muuch." Well, that's the way ol' Charlie says it. When I thank Margaret for cleaning up my mess or bringing me a Kleenex or glass of water, I'll say lightheartedly, but sincerely, "Thank you very much." Sometimes I'll give it that Charlie Brown (aka Elvis Presley) slur. . . But then most of the time I'll add my own version of, "Thank you very much, it's a pleasure doin' bidness wid-ja'." It probably doesn't make sense, but that's just the way I do it.

39 ∼ Okay, kid; that's it — that's the size of it.

Calling Margaret "kid" is just another one of those terms of endearment I use about every day. This morning, while finishing up at the breakfast table and after closing the *Free Press* (or was it the Sports section of the *News & Observer*?), I predictably said, "Okay kid, that's it — that's the size of it." What I was saying was simply, "It's all over. It's time to get up from the table and get going." I think I got the word "kid" from the old Humphrey Bogart movie, *Casablanca*. Bogart and Ingrid are saying their sad farewells when he raises his glass and says, "Here's looking at ya', kid." Sometimes I use those same words with Margaret, but most of the time it's something like, "Here's to ya', kid" or "Sure do love ya', kid." Other times I add in, "Sure do love ya', kid — I'll tell ya' that." That last "I'll tell ya' that" is just for emphasis.

Postscript: Those of you who know me and/or have read any of my books know that I sometimes I overdo my *I love you*s to Margaret. It's been that way ever since we were married. I learned that from Daddy's wise counsel. He told all three of us boys (Warren, Ely, and me) to "Be sure to tell 'um you love 'um." I've enthusiastically followed his advice — I just sometimes overdo it. But read on — there's more!

40 ∼ I sure do love ya'. You're not gonna' forget, are ya'?

I like to kid Margaret about my love for her. I guess it goes back to the *Rule of 56* which I explained in detail in my first book, *More than I Deserve*. I made it a point not to tell a girl I loved her until I was ready for marriage — and I didn't tell Margaret until the night I proposed to her at about 12:20 a.m. on Christmas morning, 1962. We were sitting in my second-row pew at Gordon

Street Christian Church all alone, of course, when I told her, "I love you and I want to marry you." I had reserved those *three little words* for Margaret all those years. I was thirty-one years old at the time, so you can understand how ready I was. The only problem was that, once I said it, I couldn't help but say it over and over again. In fact, in our early married life, I remember telling her on numerous occasions in rapid succession: "I love you, I love you, I love you," three and four times at a time. After several months I finally got the message. One day she told me with calm sincerity, "Dan, I know you love me, and I love you too. I appreciate your telling me, but you don't need to tell me *all the time*." That's when I ended up the next day counting, as objectively as I could, the number of times I told her, "I love you." It ended up being fifty-six times from the time we woke up in the morning to the time we went to sleep that night. When Warren heard the story, he kidded me by saying maybe I ought to call it the *Rule of 56* as a way of establishing the limit of "telling 'em too often." So it is today, quite often I'll kid her by saying, "I sure do love ya'. You're not gonna' forget, are ya'?" Her response is always the same. "No, I'm not gonna forget; and I love you too!"

41 ⤳ I'm just tryin' to be of help. I'm not tryin' to hurt anybody—just tryin' to help ya' 'cause I love ya'.

When I move a piece of furniture, straighten a picture, or do some other menial chore for Margaret, she'll thank me and I'll say, "I'm just tryin' to be of help. I'm not tryin' to hurt anybody—just tryin' to help ya' 'cause I love ya'." I guess it's jokingly said with a mixture of sarcasm and irony, but always good-naturedly and in a spirit of love. That's what makes all these quirky sayings so much fun. They don't mean anything—just a bunch of words, but yet they're a light means of communication. It's good that I say most of these things only to Margaret. Most other folks would think I'm too silly and a little bit off my rocker. But the good news is Margaret understands, and goes along with me with very little fanfare. She's so used to it by now, she just takes it in her stride and keeps on going.

42 ⌘ Oh-loo-oook!

Whenever our granddaughter Virginia (now 5) opens a birthday or Christmas present, I will catch myself saying, "Oh-loo-oook!" That is my way of exclaiming and adding to Virginia's surprise. She wants everybody to see her new toy. After the initial, "Oh- loo-oook" I'll generally continue in baby talk with, "That's pur-dy" or "You'll like that." Although I've used the "Oh-loo-oook" phrase from time to time over the years, it apparently lay dormant for a while until I heard Chad say it at Virginia's first or second Christmas, before she could talk. He had to help her along by focusing all our attention on that cute little doll Santa had brought her. As he held the doll up for everybody, as well as Virginia, to admire with playful pride, the words just naturally flowed in drawn-out fashion, "Oh-loo-oook!" Everybody joined in as Virginia's eyes got bigger and bigger. Ever since then, almost every time we are in Virginia's presence, that expression "Oh-loo-oook!" comes out somewhere along the way.

43 ⌘ Hey-y-y, Pod-na-a-a-a!

Warren used to call each of his grandchildren "Pod-na." It was his lighthearted way of greeting them with affection as well as friendship. It wasn't long before the greeting became standard for all the Perry clan. It was probably Stockton, Stephen, and Nathan who became the most vocal. Their hearty "Pod-na's" soon were stretched to "Pod-na-a-a-a" and sometimes when there was great jubilation and special excitement the simple "Hey, Partner" became a resounding, lengthy "Hey –y-y Pod-na-a-a-a!" We all picked up on it, and it's now standard for all of us. Sometimes I just say a simple, short, softspoken, "Hey, Partner" with almost perfect diction, but that is rare. Most of the time I'll give it that long drawn out, "Hey-y-y, Pod-na-a-a," with the emphasis on the "Pod." It makes for a right interesting greeting which all of us enjoy.

44 ⌘ Red-dio; pelly-kins; *and* herr-uh-c'n.

I guess all of us have certain words we mispronounce for one reason or another. For instance, I remember our former minister, David Alexander saying *my-rical* instead of *miracle* and *futher* instead of *further*. He would leave out the *r* when he said, "I went futher and futher down the road." Margaret and I used to chuckle when I would comment about it. Our esteemed choir director, Joanne Heath, used to pronounce it the same way. I remember way back in the fifth grade, our teacher, Miss Lanier, would say I *pa-fur* instead of *prefer*. When I remind Margaret of that, she says that's just the southern way of pronouncing it. I get teased all the time by Margaret and the children about how I mispronounce the words *radio, pelicans,* and *hurricane. Radio* usually comes out *red-dio.* To help me correct myself, I think of my friend Ray Rouse. The word then comes out *ray-dio.* When we're down at the beach and I see a group of pelicans flying by, to keep from saying *pelly-kins,* I remind myself to make it more like *pel-la cuns* (as in "Stella"-cuns) and not *pelly-kins* (as in "jelly"-kins). As far as *hurricane* is concerned, I don't know how in the world I ever came up with *herr-uh-c'n,* instead of *hurry-cane.* When I was writing this, Margaret reminded me that no one else will understand what I'm talking about other than her and the children. Private joke. Sorry 'bout that.

45 ⁓ Ohhh…they're after ya'…they're gonna' gitche one way or the other.

If your household is like ours, you are daily bombarded by telemarketers. They start as early as eight o'clock in the morning, and sometimes we get them as late as after nine o'clock at night. Every time the phone rings, we almost cringe at the thought that it might be another telemarketer—and then we look at the Caller ID screen. We are so relieved and even give a sigh when we see it's Barbara Ruth, Dinah, Ellen, Suzanne, or one of the children. I hope most people don't generally consider me a rude person, but I must admit that when the screen shows "unknown name, unknown number" or some 888 number, I have a hard time keeping my cool. Most of the time we'll either let it ring out, or turn it on and off to stop the ringing and avoid having to answer. Sometimes we'll take a chance and answer, hoping to dismiss the caller without being too rude or impolite. We've tried telling them to "take our name off your list" or "don't call us again," but it does no good. Even though I remind Margaret that, "It's somebody's son or daughter just trying to make a living," it's still irritating to both of us. What's the answer? I try to make light of the situation when the phone rings by giving a standard comment and kidding Margaret, "Ohhh…they're after ya'…they're gonna' gitche one way or the other." It probably doesn't help any, but at least it takes a little edge off the annoyance.

46 ⮑ Let's blow this firetrap.

I heard this little saying somewhere along the line when I was growing up, but the first time I specifically remember hearing it said was from my roommate at Carolina, Haywood Washburn, from Highpoint. Haywood was not only "tall, dark, and handsome," but he was also clean-cut and smart with the books. We got along great together, and one of the things I enjoyed most about him was his keen sense of humor. He had a pleasant smile and laughed a lot. In other words, he was an all around good guy. He made a lot of "cute" comments from time to time, but the one I remember most was when he said, "Let's blow this firetrap!" We were in our third-floor room at Old East dorm when one of us said something about it being time to go to supper. We were undecided as to where to go, so rather than continue our indecisiveness, Haywood ended the conversation by abruptly exclaiming, "Come on, let's blow this firetrap." The way he said it just rung a bell with me. His tone of voice was not particularly loud—just matter of fact, "Come on, let's blow this firetrap." We both laughed and I've been saying it ever since. When I'm at home and tell Margaret "Let's blow this firetrap," I think of Haywood, but also feel a little strange in referring to my beautiful home as a "firetrap." I smile when I say it, but I still have a little reservation in the back of my mind.

47 ⮑ Humburger! Humburger-roid!

I don't even know how to spell this verbal expression. It's a takeoff on *hamburger*, so I'll just give you the circumstances to show you how it came about. A lot of us have a cough from time to time due to allergies or a tickle in the throat. I eat cereal most every morning, or at least five or six times a week. I grew up eating Grape Nuts, but in the last fifteen or twenty years, I have had to change cereals because the tiny grape nuts aggravate the tickle that causes me to clear my throat, cough or even sneeze. I love almonds and peanuts and other varieties of nuts as a snack. But I know I've got to be careful, because sometimes they cause that identical throat tickle which results in the same throat clearing, coughing and/or sneezing. Many times it's just a slight clearing of the throat like my mother had and my daughter Elizabeth and son Daniel have now. At other times, it's much more pronounced, and I'm sure it's annoying to Margaret and the children and anyone else who happens to be in my company. I'll usually say the customary "Scoomy" or "Scooby-dooby," which means "excuse me" or "please excuse me." But before that, and almost simultaneous with the cough, the word "humburger" emerges. Sometimes you can only hear the "-burger" at the end of the cough. It's just a part of the cough sound. Since I don't know how to spell the sound of my cough, you'll just have to use your imagination to get the full picture. I got the word "humburger" from hearing brother Ely use it in connection with his cough when we were growing up. Sometimes when I'm really cutting up I'll make it "humburger-roid." I got the "roid" part from Cooper Taylor, my friend and former law school roommate. It's just another one of my silly quirks.

48 ～ **Wun-a-ful! Wun-a-ful!**

This is my way of poking fun at Lawrence Welk. For most of our married life it has been a tradition for Margaret and me to watch the Lawrence Welk television program on Saturday nights. I, probably more than Margaret, enjoy the "old timey" rhythms and tunes as well as the colorful costumes and showmanship of each program. All the musicians and singers give the appearance of having a good time performing and displaying their varied talents. The show is always clean and family-oriented. Our children go along with it, even though at times they think it's a little too "mushy" and overdone. We all make fun of the way Lawrence Welk pronounces certain words, "An-a-one-an-a-two-an-a." He puts an "a" at the end of most of his words which leads us to poke fun at his name by calling him "Lawrence-a Welk-a." One of the words I use quite often is his pronunciation of "Wonderful." By way of congratulating a singer or instrumentalist on his performance, he'll say, "Wun-a-ful! Wun-a-ful!" Margaret and I both have picked up on it, and make it part of our everyday vocabulary. A lot of times when I enjoy a special meal or compliment her on her progress with the piano, "I'll say, "Wun-a-ful! Wun-a-ful!" That means, of course, it's especially good.

49 ~ You're the best! Remember that, now. When you want to send the very best, send Margaret!

As you can readily see, this is a play on the Hallmark Card slogan, "When you want to send the very best, send Hallmark." It seems I tell Margaret this about every day, maybe even more than that. When I compliment her usual fine job of cooking, cleaning up, keeping the house neat, or just being her sweet self, I'll say, "You're the best! Remember that, now. When you want to send the very best, send Margaret!" Or sometimes it comes out, ". . . when *I* want to send the best, *I'll always* send Margaret." She just takes it in her stride and thinks no more about it. I guess she's so used to it; the full impact of the compliment has lost its orginial punch and effectiveness. That may be a problem with most of these silly sayings. I use them all the time because they're part of my personality. Thankfully, she hasn't had to call me down on any of these quirky quotes except in #40 when I overdid telling her "I love you." an average of about 56 times a day. It was then she told me with calm affection, "I know you love me . . . but you don't need to tell me all the time." Except for that one time about forty-five years ago, I don't believe she's ever had to tell me to ease up. To stop or slow down on any of my "quirks and quips and quotes" at this stage in life may be difficult or almost impossible. I think I'm too far over the hill and set in my ways. I guess I could do it if I had to—but I'm having too much fun to change.

50 ∽ Hold-ja-tader.

This is something I say at home, at the office, on the golf course or anywhere. That's my way of saying "Hold on now" or "Ease-up" or "Wait just a minute." If I'm on the golf course and Myron tells me to go ahead and hit, when I'm not quite ready, I say "Hold-ja-tader." One day at the office when I paused for some reason before proceeding with a matter, Miss Lin was right there and I said, "Hold-ja-tader." Not knowing what I said, or much less what it meant, she said with a puzzled look, "What did you say?" I could tell she thought it was probably one of my Korean quips, or maybe she was reading something into it that wasn't there. For whatever reason when I explained I was just telling her to wait a minute, she understood perfectly. Just another one of "Mr. Dan's" silly sayings.

51 ∽ I'm just a ham at heart!

It all started when I saw the movie, *The Jolson Story* back in the early 1940s. I was only about ten or twelve years old or so. Mother told me she thought I would really like it, so off we went to the Paramount theater to see the life story of one of the great entertainers of the early talkie movies of the 1920s and '30s. For some reason, his vaudeville and minstrel style of singing struck a permanent "yes" note in my consciousness. I remember leaving the theater "a ham at heart." I just loved the way he strutted and pranced around on the stage to the thrill of each of his audiences. I had never heard of most of his songs, but they sure had me spellbound as he dropped to his knees singing *Mammy* and *California Here I Come*. I just loved the time he interrupted a thunderous ovation by exclaiming, "You ain't heard nutin' yet!" The only way he could calm the crowd was to call upon the "Professor" to start the music to satisfy their demand for another encore. Then he'd start in with *Rosie, you are my posy, you are my heart's bouquet . . .* or *Rock-a-bye your Baby with a Dixie Mel-o-dy* and *Toot Toot Tootsie, goodbye, Toot Toot Tootsie, don't cry.* I purchased all his 78-rpm records and it wasn't long before I had all his songs memorized so I could mouth the words while mocking his various hand motions and singing style. I also saw *The Eddie Cantor Story* and learned to imitate him singing *I-da, Sweet as ap-ple ci-a-a-da, How're Ya' goina' keep um' down on the farm after they've seen Pa-ree?* and many of his other hits. I enjoyed hamming it up with the Woodberry Octet as we gleefully sang, *Dai-sy, Dai-sy, give me your answer do*! As I was writing this at the beach, July 4, 2009, I relived *The Jolson Story* a few minutes ago by talking Margaret into watching it with me on a DVD. Son Daniel started out watching with us for the first twenty minutes, but he conveniently excused himself to go upstairs and look at the ocean. It's been a long tradition of mine to watch *Yankee Doodle Dandy* during our July 4th vacation time. It's considered one of the fifty all-time great movies and stars James Cagney as George M. Cohan, the famous Broadway and patriotic composer during both World Wars. I always get a thrill when I relive his famous tap dance routine and his singing, *For it was Mary, Mary, plain as any name can be* . . . . I just can't help but visualize myself right there with ol' George M. Cohan as he sings, *I'm a Yankee Doodle Dandy, Give My Regards to Broadway,* and *You're a Grand Old Flag.* Every once in a while, Margaret or one of my friends will recognize me by commenting, "Dan, you're just a ham at heart."

52   I'm a patriot through and through!

Since my early childhood, I've always been loyal to the flag and a patriot at heart. During World War II, I remember keeping a scrapbook of all the U.S., Allied, and enemy air craft as they appeared each day in the *Free Press*. I wanted to be able to identify both friendly and enemy airplanes as well as ships and weapons. I remember how Mother and Daddy proudly displayed the two-star flag in the living room window indicating I had two brothers serving in the Armed Forces. We were so proud of both Warren and Ely as they served in naval combat in the Pacific on the battleship USS *Alabama* and the air craft carrier USS *Lexington*, respectively. I loved playing my clarinet in the Grainger High School marching band in the seventh, eighth, and ninth grades. I mostly enjoyed marching in parades as we played *Stars and Stripes Forever* and many of the John Phillip Sousa marches. When I joined the Army in 1954, I even enjoyed the rigors of basic training—or maybe I should say learning to march to the cadence count of the drill sergeant. I remember a seasoned master sergeant telling about the time when he was in formation, standing at attention, saluting the flag during the playing of the National Anthem. Some distance away, another soldier was walking across the field paying no attention to the solemn occasion. Another sergeant suddenly broke rank, ran full speed, tackled him to the ground, stood him up and made him stand at attention and salute the flag. I took pride in wearing the uniform of the U.S. Army because I knew I was representing "The land of the free and the home of the brave." I still have "chilly bumps" and at times am moved to tears when I see the colors passing by and the band playing the National Anthem. Last night, Margaret and I were watching the July 4th television special with the fireworks and patriotic music. When they played *Stars and Stripes Forever,* I found myself drawn to stand up and start directing the band. Before I knew it, I was marching to the beat while still directing—short steps, but marching steps nonetheless. Every Memorial Day and July 4th, I seem to irresistibly do the same thing. I think it must be a combination of being the "ham that I am" and "the patriot through and through" that causes this strange but predictable behavior.

53 ∽ I'm a cut-up at Rotary!

From time to time I am called upon to lead the singing at our Thursday 1 p.m. Rotary Club meeting. Suzanne Gallaher does a great job at the piano, and she usually gets someone to lead the group in singing. We used to sing two songs each week: a Rotary secular song followed by a patriotic song. There are several songs that lend themselves to cutting up, at least for some of us. John Hood and I both feel free enough to liven things up with a "Yeaaah!" or "Yu-hoo!" thrown in at just the right time. We feel that if we don't interject our own personal touches, things can sometimes be a little dull and even boring. John is a past District Governor as well as past president of the club, so he should know how to add zest and put a little gusto into a meeting. Mine just comes naturally. If the occasion calls for an exclamation, then I tend to want to give it. Some people probably think I'm a show-off and trying to draw attention to myself. It's certainly not intended, but if it is, so be it. It's all in good fun and a part of the spirit of Rotary. After the singing and before the blessing for the food, we always do the Pledge of Allegiance. That's when all the fun stops and we get dead serious, or at least I do. As a veteran of the Armed Forces, I was trained to respect the flag and give honor and dignity to the Pledge of Allegiance. This calls for standing up straight and giving full, undivided attention to the flag with the usual salute. So many times we see people casually standing on one foot with eyes directed elsewhere. Although it may be purely unintentional, it does display an air of disrespect. When saluting our flag, we need to do it with dignity and respect.

54 ⁓ I'm a Tar Heel Fan!

Ever since I can remember, I've been a Tar Heel fan. My first remembered exposure to UNC was when I was only four or five years old and Daddy drove the whole family to Chapel Hill to see the Carolina-Duke football game. We went every year to see Carolina play not only Duke, but sometimes Wake Forest and State College, as well as one time we went to a Tulane game. A lot of my memories are very vivid, even though it was more than seventy years ago: Brothers Warren and Bud (Ely Jr.) and I were in the back seat of our 1935 Chevrolet along with Aunt Susie. Daddy drove with Mother on the passenger side. Aunt Susie was always a lot of fun. Daddy used to kid her about wanting to be seen in her new dress and hat. She liked to go to the games even though she knew nothing about football. We always stopped at the halfway point in Garner for a rest stop. On my first trip, while in the restroom with Daddy, he asked me who was I pulling for. I proudly said in my wee small voice, "I'm 100% for Carolina!" Daddy used to kid me about that for years. The last eight to ten miles to the stadium was almost bumper-to-bumper traffic. It seemed like the trip took about four hours. We usually parked along Highway 54 and tailgated for our lunch of fried chicken and deviled eggs. It was a long walk to Kenan Stadium, and we were tired, but the game was worth it. That first game was traumatic for me. We had entered the gate and were working our way through the crowd right before entering the stadium itself. I was holding Daddy's hand, but somehow we got separated and all of a sudden I was all alone. Where was everybody? I started to cry, and boy did I let it be known I was lost in that noisy crowd. Finally, a nice man lifted me up where I could stand on a concrete pillow above the crowd. Almost immediately Daddy was able to see his little boy, and I was safe at last. It was in those early years that I remember learning to salute the flag with my right hand over my heart while standing at attention and singing the National Anthem. Also, that is when I learned the Carolina Alma Mater, *Hark, the sound of Tar Heel voices* . . . which ended with the fight song, "For *I'm a Tar Heel born,* and *I'm a Tar Heel bred, and when I die I'll be a Tar Heel dead* . . . . *So it's rah, rah Car-lina-lina, rah-rah Car-lina-lina* . . . . In those early games I remember all the players looking funny and hump-shouldered. I remember #81, All-American Paul Severn, and Jim "Sweet Lelonie" sweeping to his right and jumping high in the air as he passed the ball. During the war, Daddy took me to see Duke play Oregon State in the Rose Bowl game in Durham (only because it would be a once-in-a-lifetime experience). When I was in undergraduate school at Carolina, I saw just about all the home games. Charlie Justice, Art Weiner, and Bob Cox were everybody's heroes. When Carolina played Texas in the Cotton Bowl in the early '50s, one of Daddy's Texas friends sent him a telegram reading, "There is no Justice in Texas." Coach Frank McGuire brought big-time basketball to Carolina, and I well remember seeing All-American Lennie Rosenbluth and the 1957 championship team not only play, but also practice many times. I can still see Rosenbluth standing at mid-court with ball in hand and head bowed. All lights were out except for a single spotlight focused on our hero and one of the greatest ever to play at Carolina. There was a thunderous standing ovation — a truly unforgettable moment in Carolina basketball history.

I've always been a Carolina fan and always will be. Rah — Rah, Carolina! Beat Dook!

I've been a New York Yankees fan almost as long as I've been a Carolina Tar Heel fan. It all started sometime back in the 1930s when Charlie Keller was playing with the Kinston Eagles baseball team. Daddy started me out early, seeing not only the Tar Heels play football, but also the Eagles play baseball. I remember both Daddy and brother Ely, Jr. talking about how good Charlie Keller was—and I remember seeing him knocking balls over the fence. His nickname was "King-Kong" Keller, because he was known to be a home-run hitter. It wasn't long before the New York Yankees had him playing in the big leagues. My recollection is that Charlie played right field along with the immortal Joe DiMaggio in centerfield. Beginning about 1938 and into the '40s, I knew all the players and the batting averages both for the Yankees as well as the Eagles (now the Indians). In those days, the Yankees were perennial world champions, and I was one of their top fans. Ely, Jr. and I would check the *Free Press* each afternoon to see how the Yankees and the Eagles were doing. I also followed Ted Williams of the Boston Red Sox as well as a lot of other players from various teams. My "tombstone buddy" and across the street friend, Z.A. Collins, and I saw a lot of the Eagles' games together. One of the players we had fun with was Pete Peistrack who changed his name to Pete Peters (because his last name was hard to spell, I guess). Pete Peters played third base and was known to carry on a lot of chatter as he tended his position. For the longest time, Z.A. and I thought he was saying, "Shoot the *loddy hossy* to me, babe." Finally, we figured out he actually was saying, "Let's have *a lot of hustle* out here, babe." Other memorable Eagles were Roy Kennedy, Bob Cohen, and John Tepedino, who was nick named "Tripledino" because he was famous for hitting so many triples. He had a brother, Frank Tepedino, who was also quite good. The modern name for the Kinston Eagles is the Kinston Indians, for they are now a farm team of the Cleveland Indians. After more than seventy years, I still get a lot of pleasure following the Yankees and the Indians.

My brother Warren started me off playing golf when I was six years old. He gave me a chipper called a "33 club." After several nine-holes, I graduated to carrying a small bag with several odd clubs—a "brassie" (two-wood) and a "niblick" (five-iron) and a putter along with my 33 club. I've always loved golf and have enjoyed playing and following the "big boys" on the P.G.A. tour. Sam Snead was always a favorite of mine. When I was at Carolina, I remember following Harvie Ward's amateur career. It was about that time that everybody was talking about Arnold Palmer of Wake Forest and how good he was. When he turned pro after graduation, I followed his career in the newspaper and magazines, as well as on radio and television. Known for his charisma, he was my big hero. Jack Nicklaus came along about ten years later and was an instant hit. In April 1963, Margaret and I were returning from our honeymoon in Jamaica. We (or I should say I) made a point of stopping by Augusta to catch the final day of the Masters. I believe it only cost about $15.00 to get in. We were rewarded with an unforgettable sight—Jack Nicklaus strolling up the 18th fairway to the applause and cheers of the adoring crowd. He was about to win his first Masters. He had already acquired the nickname "The Golden Bear." I remember him being a little chubby, but gracious and modest as he acknowledged his victory. He went on to win eighteen major tournaments and, according to my good friend Roy Jones, it is a record that will never be broken—not even by Tiger Woods. After Tiger won his sixth major, he was really on a roll and Roy and I were at the Kinston Country Club talking about it. I was a Tiger fan and I "bet" Roy he would one day beat Nicklaus' record. Roy responded by saying "when Tiger wins nineteen majors, I'll cook you a steak dinner." Every once in a while I'll kid Roy by saying, "Remember now, I want mine medium rare." Roy still doesn't believe Tiger will do it, but I still keep reminding him of his steak promise. As of this writing, Tiger has won fourteen majors, and I'm convinced he'll win at least five more, and probably even more that that. I'm a Tiger fan, and I believe he'll go down as the greatest golfer who ever lived.

Postscript: My tribute to Tiger Woods was written several months before his "fall from grace" in the public eye. His loose moral standards were a shock to me as well as the entire sports world. This has led many former admirers to lose heart and focus their attention on his weaknesses rather than his strengths. He serves as a constant reminder that "even the best of us are subject to fall." He is one of the many public figures who has fallen victim to the world's system of lust, pride, and greed. They range from athletes to lawyers, doctors to politicians, and even preachers. Before we judge Tiger too harshly, we need to examine our own lives and recognize that none of us is beyond the downward pull of worldly living. We all need to keep our guard up so as to avoid a similar fate. By the time this book is published, I pray that Tiger will have admitted and repented of his sin, because that's exactly what it is. We may want to minimize it by calling it a "shortcoming" or "indiscretion," but the truth is, in the eyes of our eternal God, it's sin. The only way Tiger can get back to being the greatest golfer who ever lived is to put all this behind him and move on with his life. He needs to get it out in the open and ask God's forgiveness as well as that of his family and friends, and the public in general. Only then will he be able to concentrate his attention on the game he loves so much. I am praying he will do just that. I believe he will go on to win many more golf tournaments, including at least five or more majors. I'm still a Tiger Woods fan and wish him the best as he moves forward.

PART TWO

Meaningful Thoughts

*Some of these thoughts are my own,
others have been gleaned from respected
mentors—all are meaningful to me.*

57 ~ **Thank you, Lord. Thank you, thank you, thank you!**

This is an expression I use every day in one form or another. Many days I catch myself saying it continuously, numerous times a day. I have a habit of counting my blessings quite frequently. It's just a natural response as I see the abundance of God's blessings upon me and my family. If we make ourselves aware of God's goodness day in and day out, over the years, and if we can just understand that everything we have and everything we are is a blessing from our heavenly Father, what a difference it makes. All of our physical and spiritual blessings come from the God of the Universe, the God who created us and sustains us. He gives us not only "our daily bread," but so much more. How can we help but thank Him? In the last couple of years, I have renewed my friendship with Chuck Haywood, a former classmate at Woodberry Forest where we graduated together in 1949. We were also classmates at UNC in Chapel Hill, but for some reason after our freshman year, our paths seldom crossed. Since our 1953 graduation, we have seen each other only a couple of times until two years ago. I always knew Chuck as a man of integrity and all around "good guy." When our friendship was renewed, mostly by telephone, I was impressed in a new and marvelous way. Every time we talk, he repeatedly gives thanks for his many blessings. He emphasizes that, "I can't ever tell you how much God has blessed me — and in so many ways!" Chuck and I both have learned that, even in the midst of adversity and when life really gets tough, we can and should count our blessings and say, "Thank you, Lord! Thank you, thank you, thank you!"

58 ~ **Christianity is not a religion — it's a relationship.**

I first heard this expression from Dick Day, a representative of Campus Crusade for Christ. It was sometime in the early 1970s, and I had heard he would be speaking to the students of Parrott Academy in Kinston. Although we had never met, four things drew me to hear him speak: first, he was the brother of my friend Debbie Thompson (now Wallace); second, he was a representative of Campus Crusade for Christ; third, somebody told me about it and encouraged me to go; and fourth, it was the indwelling Holy Spirit who drew me to attend. I just knew I had to be there, even though he would be speaking to a group of students. It turned out to be a life-changing experience for me, because it was the first time I had heard the expression, "Christianity is not a religion—it's a relationship." He went on to explain, "It's not religion we need, it's a relationship—a relationship with Jesus Christ." His words really made sense, and I've never forgotten them. In fact, I began to realize that all of life is based upon relationships, whether they are family relationships, work relationships, political relationships, or whatever. But the most important relationship of all is our relationship with the Son of God, Jesus Christ. Without that proper relationship, we miss out on what life is all about. Without a proper relationship with Jesus, we cannot enter God's heavenly kingdom. That's not what I say; it's what God Himself says through His Word. Without a proper relationship with Jesus, we can't have a truly meaningful relationship with family and friends. By *truly meaningful*, I mean a relationship the way God designed it to be, which is better than anything the world can offer.

59 ⤳ Love is the greatest thing in the world.

No doubt many people over the years have used this expression, but the first "official" time I remember seeing it in print was in Henry Drummond's sermon, *The Greatest Thing in the World*, first published in about 1883. Later it was reduced to booklet form as a best seller. I read it first in 1956, when Daddy gave me a copy and encouraged me to read it and live by it. It was about that time he began giving a pocket edition to each Eagle Scout going through the Caswell District. He always referred to it as *The Little Red Book* and took pleasure in challenging the new Eagles to base all their thoughts, words, and deeds on *The Greatest Thing in the World*. The book itself is a dissertation by Drummond based on Saint Paul's 13th chapter of First Corinthians, the great biblical chapter on love. As did Paul, Drummond contrasts love with the other great things of the world. Next, he analyses it by breaking it down into its component parts; and then he defends it and singles out love as being the *summum bonum*—the supreme good. Here again, Paul's immortal words in verse 13, "And now abideth faith, hope, love, these three; but the greatest of these is Love." Daddy told me before he died that he passed out about nine thousand copies of The Little Red *Book* during his lifetime. Wherever he traveled, whether to Europe or around the world, whenever he made a talk in Kinston or elsewhere, he always carried a supply of *The Little Red Book* to share with his audience. Henry Drummond challenged his readers to join him in "reading this chapter once a week for the next three months. A man did that once and it changed his life. Will you do it?" Soon after Daddy gave me my copy, I memorized all thirteen verses of the 13th chapter of First Corinthians and repeated them daily for quite a while. I still do it from time to time, and it no doubt has had a profound impact on my life.

60 ⤳ You don't need legal advice—you need spiritual advice.

Through the years in my law practice, I represented quite a few clients with marital problems. Sometimes the husband or wife came alone, wondering what to do about their domestic problems. Other times, they both came. They were seeking legal advice as to their rights. As I listened to their problems, first one side and then the other, in most cases I advised that each party would need a lawyer if there was to be a legal battle. I couldn't represent both sides. But almost always the root of their problems was a spiritual matter rather than a legal matter. I knew in my heart that the best advice I could give was to make Jesus the common denominator between them. He was the answer to all their problems. If each party would put Jesus, instead of themselves, first in their lives, they would begin to see the error of their ways. Love and sharing instead hostility and selfishness would be the central rule. I found this to be true in most every case. One of the problems many of my clients faced was that they didn't believe Jesus was the answer. They had little spiritual background in their family rearing to give them a basis to believe in

Jesus. They had heard about Him, but they didn't understand that He was available to everyone who believed in Him. One of the things I tried to help them see was that Jesus was indeed real. He could and would help them work out their problems. It was a matter of priority: each party putting *Jesus first, you second, and me third.* I don't know the success rate that this advice yielded, but I do know that many marriages were healed by making Jesus the common denominator. I truly believe that if all couples would seek spiritual advice first, there would be little or no need for legal advice.

61 ⤳ When you're down and out, that's the very time you need to praise God and thank Him.

Alan Armstrong, minister of music at Faith Fellowship Church, often substituted for Randy Spaugh when Randy was on vacation. In one of his first sermons, Alan reminded us that we are to *praise* God for who He is and *thank* Him for what He has done for us. Praise and thanksgiving are the essence of effective worship. The problem is a lot of us think praise and thanksgiving should mostly be reserved only for Sunday morning worship service. The more mature Christian, however, will make praise and thanksgiving a daily practice—every day, many times a day. Paul tells us to "Pray without ceasing, in everything give thanks; for this is the will of God in Christ Jesus for you" (1 Thessalonians 5:17-18). The same is true of praise. Not only should we pray and give thanks in all things, but we should also praise God in all things. One of the greatest living advocates of praise and thanksgiving I know is Merlin Carrothers. That's the essence of his entire ministry. He has written numerous books and pamphlets on the subject of praise. As an Army chaplain, he first wrote *Prison to Praise,* followed by *Power in Praise,* and *Answers to Praise.* He spoke to our Full Gospel Business Men's Fellowship meeting back in the early 1970s, and left a lasting impression on all of us. In all of his books, he gives example after example of how, when we praise God in the midst of our darkest trials, the Lord takes our praise and turns it into miraculous blessings. I have tried to learn that lesson over the years and can testify that it really works. When we're down and out, the world system tells us to gripe and grumble. That's exactly the opposite of what our heavenly Father would have us do. Especially when we're down and out, that's the very time He wants us to praise Him and thank Him for all He's done for us. I challenge you to praise Him and thank Him in all situations. Try it; you'll see Him do a miraculous work in your life.

62 ～ Adversity strengthens character.

This was what fellow attorney Marion Parrott told me when I failed the bar exam the first time. Even though I knew it wasn't the end of the world when I heard the devastating news, I definitely needed some encouragement. Mother and Daddy, as well as brothers Warren and Ely, helped reinforce my belief that things would eventually work out for the best. The most memorable encouragement I got, however, was what Marion told me. He said "adversity strengthens character." He went on to relate how many well-known and famous leaders overcame their adversities and went on to live productive and rewarding lives. I have given that advice to many others throughout the years. Of course, it all boils down to a matter of attitude and how we view our adversities. Disappointment and adversity come to all of us in one way or another. I have learned that the key to handling adversity is to look at it from God's perspective. I'm reminded of how Joseph responded to the ill treatment his jealous brothers gave him by selling him into slavery. Joseph was taken off to Egypt never to be heard of again — at least that's what his brothers thought and hoped. It turned out that Joseph rose to a level second only to Pharaoh in authority over all of Egypt. God used him to save the people of Israel from the destruction of the famine. When first confronting his brothers, he told them, "... you meant evil against me; but God meant it for good... (Genesis 50:20). When we are able to look at our adversities from God's perspective, we can see that the world and Satan "meant it for evil, but God meant it for good." This is when we can reap the benefits from Marion's statement that *adversity strengthens character.*

63 ⮑ Everything that happens to a Christian is filtered through God's fingers of love.

I've heard this statement used many times, but I think I first heard it from Kay Arthur. It's an amazing statement, but I'm convinced it's true. Think about it. God loves us all—even the worst sinners, but it seems He has a special love for His own children—those who have placed their trust in His only begotten Son as their Lord and Savior. You might relate it to the love of an earthly father for his own children. The Bible says that even though a father should love everybody, even his enemies, he has a special love for his own son. As the earthly father wants the best for his son, so our heavenly Father wants the best for each and every one of His children. To make that point, the Bible poses these questions, "O what man is there among you who, if his son asks for bread, will give him a stone? Or if he asks for a fish will give him a serpent" (Matt. 7:9-10). We need to remember that, even though God allows us a certain degree of freedom to make our own choices, He ultimately is in charge and in control of our lives. Even though we make certain decisions that lead down the wrong path resulting in adversities and even broken lives, God is still in control. He is aware of everything that happens to us, whether good or bad, whether for our benefit or detriment. In His sovereign and divine plan for our lives, He can turn everything bad into everything good. He can make even the worst of circumstances result in something good in the overall scheme of things. He always has our best interest in mind. After all, He is our heavenly Father and we are His children—and He wants the best for us. That's why we can be assured that everything that happens to us as His children is filtered through His fingers of love.

64 ⮑ The Lord wants us to yield our lives and be willing to be led by Him.

I've been journaling since January 1, 1999, and it has been a marvelous experience. Each morning when I enter into the quietness of my home study, the first thing I do is pull out my *Private Journal* and begin communicating with my heavenly Father. I always start with, "Dear Lord," and then proceed to write what's on my mind. Sometimes my words are in the form of a prayer regarding some situation or need that has captured my attention. Sometimes, they are in the form of a Psalm of praise and thanksgiving. Before the end of the page, I usually spend a lot of time counting my blessings and naming them one by one. When I began writing my first book, *More Than I Deserve*, in 2006, I specifically asked the Lord to guide me every step of the way. He had convinced me that it was His will that I write the book. It became clear to me that my job was "to be willing to be led." God had laid on my heart that He had a job for me to do. He knew I wanted to do His will, for in His sovereign plan for my life, He had led me in that direction. It was only natural that my prayer would be, *Lord, I know you want me to write this book. I'm willing to be led to do and write exactly what you want me to say.* That has become my daily prayer as I have written each of my books. The Lord has a central message He wants to convey to each of my readers—and that's the message of salvation. He wants to use me as an instrument of His peace and grace and mercy. *Lord, if that's what You want me to do; I'm willing to be led. You lead and I will follow.*

65 ⟋ A man of God in the will of God is immortal until his work on earth is done.

I first heard this statement on 100.3 FM radio several years ago in a Bible study by David Jeremiah. When he said it, I was on the floor doing my morning stretching exercises and didn't have access to paper and pencil, so I asked Margaret to remember it and write it down, which she did. I wanted to reflect on those most interesting words. Jeremiah went on to explain that the objective of all of us should be to be in God's will. He has a divine plan for each of us, and He wants us to be led by Him as we fall in line with His will for our lives. But what did he mean by his statement that if we are in God's will we are *immortal* until our work on earth is done? That was what was so intriguing to me. *Immortal?* It sounded to me like he was saying yes, we are immortal until our work is done. If this is true, it means not only that we *will not die* but also we *cannot die* until God is through with us. And that's what David Jeremiah

51

was explaining to us. Of course, it all hinges on whether or not we are in God's will. If God has a job for us to do, He will not allow us to die before our work is completed. In my study of God's sovereignty, I have learned that the ultimate control of each of us is in His hands. He is God and He can do what He wants in order to prolong our lives for any reason. He not only *can*, he *will* do it. In His omnipotence, He can let me live to age seventy-eight (which is my age now) or one hundred and eight. It's entirely up to Him. As long as He has a job for me to do, He will provide the energy and wherewithal to get the job done. Someone asked me how many books I intend to write. My answer was, "I'll just keep writing until He's through with me." This is my fourth book. Whether He has any more in mind is up to Him. I have a feeling He has a bunch more for me to write.

66 ⁓ To see God's hand in everything makes life a great adventure.

I read this statement in a *Daily Bread* devotional a couple years ago and have kept it in the forefront of my mind ever since. To understand that life can be a great adventure is not only exciting, but it's also energizing. Life does not have to be drudgery. Even in the midst of pain, sorrow, and disappointment it can still be exciting, even adventurous. How can that be? Under the world system, it would follow that adversity brings discomfort, frustration, and discouragement. How in the world can we find adventure and excitement in adversity and misfortune? It's all a matter of attitude and perspective. As I have come to get a glimpse of God's sovereignty and His loving nature, I have come to realize that He loves each of His children and wants the best for each of us. He's also in control of our lives. Just because bad things happen to us, this does not mean our heavenly Father has forgotten us or is causing those adversities to come into our lives without a reason. As a matter of fact I'm convinced that everything that happens to us, God allows for a reason—and it's a good reason, designed to develop our character and draw us closer to Him. He wants us to trust Him and be dependent on Him to run our lives. Our basic problem is that we want to run our own lives and be independent of God.

Our goal should be to reach that point in our lives where we can give up our will for His will, and learn to be led by Him rather than trying to have Him follow us. That's when life takes on new meaning—that's when we can begin to see God's hand in everything that happens to us—and that's when we can experience the excitement of knowing that life is indeed a great adventure.

67 ❧ God's number one priority for His children is that we have an intimate relationship with Him.

When we accept the Son of God as our Lord and Savior, we are adopted into God's family—we become a child of God by adoption. When I received Christ at the age of twelve, I was "born again," and automatically became God's son. He was my heavenly Father. He not only had a plan for my life, but He also set high expectations and priorities so I could better follow His will and be the person He designed me to be. To help me know His will, He made it clear that I needed to develop a close, personal relationship with Him. Later on in my Christian walk, I realized that having that close, intimate relationship with Him was His number one priority for me as His son. I also learned that the degree of impact of my life would be determined by my degree of intimacy with Him. The more intimate my relationship with my heavenly Father, the more impact my life would have as an influence for good. It took me many years to come to the realization that a Sunday morning Christian was not what my heavenly Father had in mind for me as His son. He wants so much more for all His children. As beneficial as a Sunday morning worship service may be, it is not enough to develop the type of Father/son relationship He has in mind. There's a major difference between a casual, or surface, relationship and a close, intimate relationship. The more intimate we are in our relationship with God, the easier it is for us to discern His highest will for us. Why settle for second best? If your friends think you are too fanatical, so be it! I'm convinced that, in the end, it will pay off with amazing dividends and a rewarding life.

68 ∾ **Sufficient quality time with our heavenly Father is essential to having an intimate relationship with Him.**

We learned this in one of our Bible studies. It stands to reason that to have a close personal relationship with another person you've got to spend time with him. The same is true if we are to know our heavenly Father; we've got to spend time with Him. For emphasis, we said it's not simply *time* with Him, its *quality time*, and not simply quality time, its *sufficient quality time*. If any of those three elements is missing, our relationship with God is not what it can be and should be. We've all heard people boast about their going to church each week as a means of trying to impress us with their spirituality. Regular church attendance is a good thing, but one hour a week is not enough time with the Lord to develop a close, personal relationship with Him. Reading God's Word haphazardly while halfway watching television is too much of a distraction to develop such a relationship with the Father. What kind of quality time are we talking about? I believe the best quality time is *quiet time*, free from any distractions — no radio, no television, no newspaper, no telephone, nothing to distract us from giving our full focus and attention to the loving presence of our heavenly Father. The prophet Isaiah refers to it as, "In quietness and confidence shall be your strength" (Isaiah 30:15). What do we mean by *sufficient* quality time? Obviously it's not a hit or miss, or an occasional type of thing. You can't expect to develop an intimate, personal relationship with God by spending fifteen minutes a week with Him. I have found that it's best to have quality communication with Him on a *daily basis*. The more quality time we spend in His presence, the more intimate our relationship will be with Him, and the better we will fulfill His highest priority for our lives.

69 ∾ **God's number one purpose for His children is that we be conformed to the image and likeness of His Son.**

If we understand and profit from having an intimate relationship with our heavenly Father, He will make it clear that His number one purpose for each of His children is that we be conformed to the image and likeness of His only begotten Son. When we accept Jesus as our Lord and Savior, we are adopted into God's family—we become His children. So what is His number one purpose for each of His children? He wants us to live our lives with His Son Jesus as our role model. In other words, He wants us to be conformed to the image and likeness of Jesus. Jesus was begotten by His heavenly Father. You and I were begotten by our earthly father. Jesus is perfect in every way because He was God in the flesh, the God-man. You and I are born in sin and have a sin nature. When we accept Christ as having paid our sin debt in full, we are given a new nature—the sinless nature of Christ Jesus. Our position in Christ is that we are sinless like Christ. But in practice, as long as we continue living on this earth, our flesh will be at war with our new nature. We will continue to sin, at least in our thoughts, even though outwardly we may impress others as being "good guys," with only an occasional, insignificant sin. God is interested in conforming our entire being into the sinless image and likeness of His Son Jesus. He knows His work in us will not be completed during out earthly existence, but it's still His number one purpose for us. Our job is to daily practice yielding our lives to His calling and purpose. The more intimate our relationship is with Him, and the more we yield to His leading, the more His purpose for us will be manifested in our lives. Have you ever noticed that the longer a married couple lives together in a close relationship and looks at each other on a daily basis over the years, the more they sometimes begin to look alike? In like manner, the more we look at Jesus and live with Him on an intimidate daily basis, the more we begin to look like Him in our daily actions. At the end of our earthly lives and when we enter into God's heavenly kingdom, His purpose of conforming us into the image and likeness of Jesus will be complete. We will then live with Him forever and ever throughout all eternity.

70 ✺ If you were accused of being a Christian, would there be enough evidence to convict you?

It was Billy Graham who posed that question in Chapel Hill back in the 1950s. That was the first time I heard it, but have been challenged by it many times since. What a soul-searching question for all Christians to consider! An honest appraisal of my own life reveals at least some evidence of my being a believer in Jesus Christ. I read the Bible, go to church, and do all the things that a normal Christian does, but is that enough proof to convict me of being a follower of Christ? A lot of "good people" call themselves Christians and do a lot of surface things that would at least be enough evidence to bring a bill of indictment if brought before a grand jury. As a lawyer I'm aware that a bill of indictment is not enough evidence to warrant a conviction in a court of law with a jury of twelve of my peers. The test for conviction is whether or not the prosecutor can present enough evidence to prove to the jury *beyond a reasonable doubt* that I, or any of us, fall within the definition of being Christian. What proof is there to convince the jury *beyond a reasonable doubt*? Mere proof of our belief in Jesus is not enough. Plenty of people, including Satan, believe in Jesus. But the real question and true test is whether we *follow* Him. Are we embarrassed when the going gets rough? When we face extreme adversity and persecution, do we stand up and let ourselves be counted as followers of Christ? No one reading this book has ever been tested to the point of martyrdom. Would we give in to the pressure of facing death for the cause of Christ? We may talk a big game, but do we walk the walk sufficiently to be convicted of being a Christian beyond a reasonable doubt? A lot of us would fail that test.

PART THREE

Favorite Bible Verses

Following is a sample of some verses of Scripture
that have special meaning for me.

71 ⁓ **"And you shall know the truth and the truth shall make you free." John 8:32**

The world system would have us believe a lie. The Bible would have us believe the truth. I am convinced that if we seek to know the truth as presented in God's Word, we shall indeed come to know the truth, and we will be made free of the lie as offered by the world. Truth is what we all need, for it is the essence of a meaningful life. Verse 36 goes on to tell us that Jesus Himself is the truth who sets us free: "Therefore if the Son makes you free, you shall be free indeed." Jesus' listeners were offended because they considered themselves in bondage to no one, but Jesus insisted that only faith in Him could free anyone from the power of sin. Jesus is the source of truth, the perfect standard of what is right. Only Jesus can free us from our continued slavery to sin and from the deception by Satan. It is only through faith in Jesus that we can know the truth, because *He is the truth* and it is only He who gives us eternal life. It is interesting to observe that when Jesus sets us free, He does not give us freedom to do what we want, but rather freedom to follow God's plan for our lives. Our job is to seek to serve God. It is then that Jesus' perfect truth frees us to be all that God means for us to be. This may seem strange and even foreign to the undiscerning heart, but once you ponder it and allow the indwelling Holy Spirit to enlighten you, He will reveal this amazing truth to your spirit. Yes, Jesus is the truth and only He can make you free from the binding force of sin.

72 ⁓ **"Jesus said to him, 'I am the way, the truth, and the life. No one comes to the Father except through me.'" John 14:6**

Our Father who art in heaven is holy, righteous, and sinless. He is perfect in every way, and for anyone who expects to live eternally in heaven with Him, he too must be perfect and without sin. Jesus makes it clear in this verse that the only way we can be made righteous so as to come to the Father is through Him, the Son of God. In today's culture it seems fashionable to believe that there are many roads that lead to the Father. Why would God make it so restrictive? Why would He make the path so narrow? If He wants all of us to go to heaven, why does He make it so hard to get there? A close look at the context of God's Word reveals that He's not making it hard to get there, but is making it restrictive. Jesus tells us in Matthew 7:13-14: "You can enter God's kingdom only through the narrow gate. The highway to hell is broad . . . . But the gateway to life is very narrow and the road is difficult . . . ."(NLT) He further tells us in John 10:9: "Yes, I am the gate. Those who come in through Me will be saved . . . ." (NLT) When Jesus says the gate is narrow that leads to eternal life, He's not saying it's difficult to become a Christian, but He is saying there's only one way. When He says the "road is difficult," He's telling us plainly that once you decide to enter the gate, the Christian life is the opposite of easy; it's "difficult." In further context of God's Word we learn that the Christian walk is not just difficult, but it is impossible to live in our own strength. It is the indwelling Holy Spirit living His life through us who makes the Christian life possible. Why is believing in Jesus the only way to heaven? Because He alone died for our sins to offer us the way to make us right before God. Walking on life's road with Jesus may not be popular, but it is true and right and the rewards are beyond fantastic.

73 ⟶ "All Scripture is given by inspiration of God, and is profitable for doctrine, for reproof, for correction, for instruction in righteousness." 2 Timothy 3:16

It is my understanding that the true Greek translation for the words, "given by inspiration of God" is that all Scripture is "God-breathed" or "inspired by God." The Bible is not a human book, it is not a collection of stories, fables, myths, or merely human ideas about God as some would have us believe. It came about through the work of the Holy Spirit. God revealed His person and plan for life through certain believers, and they wrote down what He inspired them to write. God had a message for His people and He used human beings to deliver that message according to His instructions. Each writer wrote from his own personal, historical, and cultural contexts. The footnote in my *New Living Translation* says that, "Although they used their own minds, talents, language, and style, they wrote what God wanted them to write." Scripture is completely trustworthy because God was in control of its writing. Its words are entirely authoritative for our faith and life. The Bible is "God-breathed." It says that all Scripture is "profitable for doctrine, for reproof, for correction, for instruction in righteousness." In other words, as verse 17 says, "God used it to prepare and equip His people to do every good work."(NLT). God's Word is our plumb line and standard for testing everything else that claims to be true. It is our safeguard against false teaching and our source of guidance for how we should live our lives. It is interesting to note that the Bible is our only source of knowledge about how we can be saved. If we read and study it faithfully, we can discover God's truth and become confident and effective in our life and faith.

74 ∽ "For the time is coming when people will no longer listen to sound doctrine and wholesome teaching. They will follow their own desires and will look for teachers who will tell them whatever their itching ears want to hear." 2 Timothy 4:3 (NLT)

During my lifetime I have witnessed this prophecy come to fruition. It's happening all over America and throughout the world. Paul was advising young Timothy to "preach the Word" while they are receptive. In looking down the road, Paul was telling him there will come a time when they will not listen. In verse 4, he tells Timothy, "They will reject the truth and chase after myths." Today we live in a time of affluence and "designer doctrine," when people pick and choose what to believe. We tend to base our choices on our own desires and preferences. We won't listen to "sound doctrine and wholesome teaching." Instead, we "reject the truth and chase after myths." You can see this everywhere — from liberal churches to university campuses. In our minds we think the dusty Bible is worn out and old-fashioned. We are smart and well educated enough on our own that we don't need the Bible to guide us. The *New Living Translation Bible* footnote points out that such people have at least three things in common: "(1) They do not tolerate the truth.... (2) They reject the truth .... (3) They gather new points to suit their selfish desires." Such teachers have a following because they are telling people "whatever they want to hear." False teachers can be found any and everywhere—even in churches. Maybe we are more correct to say *especially in churches*. How can we identify a false teacher? First, we need to keep a clear mind in every situation, and then test and compare what is said in God's Word. What does the Bible say? Therein lies the truth, because it is the truth.

75 ⟋ **"Beware lest anyone cheat you through philosophy and empty deceit, according to the basic principles of the world and not according to Christ." Colossians 2:8**

Here again, Paul is warning his readers to beware of false teachers who will deceive you with worldly thinking. So many times human ideas and experiences sound good and truthful. Paul himself was a gifted philosopher, so he was not condemning philosophy itself. What he was condemning were teachings that credit humanity and not Christ as being the truth and the answer to life's problems. Under the inspiration of the Holy Spirit, Paul was led to write that we should keep our eyes on Christ and God's Word and not on mere philosophy and human thinking. As a first-year Woodberry Forest boy in 1946, I heard a seminar speaker pose the question, "What is philosophy?" Louis Howard, one of my classmates, defined philosophy as "a way of thinking," and I'd say Louis had it right. It is *a way* of thinking. That doesn't mean it's necessarily the truth, because it's man's thinking, and therefore it is subject to error. Why does Paul say we should test out thoughts "according to Christ" and not to the "basic principles of the world?" He goes on to explain in verses 9 and 10, "For in Him [Christ] dwells all the fullness of the Godhead bodily; and you are complete in Him, who is the head of all principality and power." In other words, when we have Christ we have everything we need for salvation and right-living. He is "the way, the truth and the life," and if we know Christ Jesus, we don't need to seek God by means of other religions, cultures, or unbiblical philosophers as the Colossians did, and as so many of us in today's affluent culture are doing as well. Christ is the unique source of knowledge and power for the Christian life, and He alone holds the answer to the true meaning of life—because *He is life*. That's what the Bible says and I believe it.

76 ∽ "The grass withers, the flowers fade, but the Word of our God stands forever." Isaiah 40:8

The Bible has been attacked by critics for centuries. In the early days, they even tried to burn all the copies. In today's society they're trying to remove every reference to it in schools and public places. In the previous verses, 6 and 7, the prophet Isaiah compares people to grass and flowers that wither and fade away. What he's saying is that we are all mortal, but God's Word is constant and "stands forever." I, for one, would rather bank my life on the trustworthiness of the Bible than on the "empty deceit" of the philosophies of man. In time, such humanistic thought will wither and fade away, but the wisdom of the Bible will remain and "stand forever." There are two things that are immortal—that will never die: the human soul, and God's Word. Many people do not understand that a person's soul, whether saved or unsaved, will live forever, either in the presence of the Almighty God, or separated from Him. The soul of a person does not die. It will live eternally either in heaven or in hell—one or the other. There is no escape. How do we know this? The Bible tells us so. During our earthly existence our Maker, our heavenly Father, wants us to get to know Him so He can give us *the life* He promises through His Son. The Bible says that only through our faith in His Son Jesus can we receive both abundant life on earth and eternal life in heaven. That's what God's Word says, and that's why He wants us to read it. God speaks to us through the reading of His Word. That's why we need to make it a daily practice to read and study it, so as to be able to listen intently to God's communication with us. He wants the best for all His children, and it is through the reading and understanding of His Word that we come to know His very best.

77   "The Word of God is living and powerful and sharper than any two-edged sword, piercing even to the division of soul and spirit, and of joints and marrow, and is a discerner of the thoughts and intents of the heart." Hebrews 4:12

Bible study leader Kay Arthur explains why God's Word is called the Sword. She says it is, "because of its piercing ability, operating with equal effectiveness upon sinners, saints, and Satan. It has the power to reach to the innermost parts of one's personality, and discerns [judges] the innermost thoughts." The Bible is not simply a collection of words from God. More importantly, it's His vehicle for communicating His thoughts and ideas to us, his children. It has been referred to as God's love letter to His children. The Bible is His Word. It's not dead by any stretch of the imagination. It is alive and powerful! It's life-changing and dynamic as it works in our lives. Why is it alive? Because God Himself not only brought it into existence, but also the Spirit of God brings its message to life in our hearts. It's God power that provokes change in our lives. With the precision of a surgeon's knife, it reveals who we are and who we are not. It has the power to penetrate the core of our moral and spiritual life. As we read and study its essence, we see that it discerns what is within us, both good and evil. If we but give it a chance, it will shape our lives. It will require decisions to be made for our good and eternal well-being. The problem is that most of us don't make the effort to genuinely spend *sufficient quality time* to seek out its message to us. We evidently don't believe it is "living and powerful and sharper than any two-edged sword." If we did, we would spend more time reading it.

78   "For God so loved the world that He gave His only begotten Son, that whoever believes in Him should not perish but have everlasting life." John 3:16

This verse is the "mother of all Scripture," for it encapsulates the essence of the entire Word of God. The Bible is all about God's love for all mankind. The central figure is His Son, Jesus, the Christ. The word *Christ* is the Greek title given to the Son of God. It means the "Anointed One," the "long-awaited

Messiah," the "Savior of the world." Throughout history as revealed in the Old Testament, the people of Israel had been anticipating the arrival of the Messiah whom God had promised to save them from the bondage of sin. Verse 15 tells us that, "Whoever believes in Him shall not perish but have eternal life." When I was growing up in the church, I remember being taught at an early age that "God is love" and one of the first Scripture verses we all memorized was John 3:16. I later learned that this is what the "Good News" and the Gospel, is all about. When God sent His only begotten Son into the world to die and pay the ultimate price for our sins, He was setting the pattern for true love and the basis for all love. John later confirmed this when he said, "Greater love has no one than this, than to lay down one's life for his friends" (John 15:13). When you love someone dearly, you are willing to give freely, to the point of self sacrifice. God loved all the world so much that He was willing to pay the highest price He could pay—the life of His own Son—to save us from our sins. When we accept the Good News and share it with others, we are spreading God's love and fulfilling the "Great Commission" commanded by Jesus to, "Go into all the world and preach the Good News to everyone. Anyone who believes and is baptized will be saved. But anyone who refuses to believe will be condemned" (Mark 16:16-17) (NLT).

79 ∽ "For by grace you have been saved through faith, and that not of yourselves; it is the gift of God." Ephesians 2:8

This is one of the great passages making it clear that there is nothing we can do by our good works to be saved from the penalty of sin. When we believe in Jesus and trust in the fact that He became our substitute when He died for our sins, we became righteous in the eyes of God. It is God's work, not ours. Our salvation is a gift from God and has nothing to do with any "good works" we may have done. It's all up to God, not we ourselves. All we have to do is accept His gift. That concept is hard for many people to understand. They think they've got to do something—*at least something*—to earn their salvation. This verse tells us we can take no credit whatsoever. If we had to do anything, it wouldn't be a gift. Verses 9 and 10 of the *New Living Translation* go on to explain: "Salvation is not a reward for the good things we have done, so none of us can boast from it. For we are God's master piece. He has created us anew in Christ Jesus, so we can do the good things He planned for us long ago." So it is that when we receive Christ by accepting His free gift of salvation, our response is one of gratitude and praise to the giver of all good gifts. He will then lead us to seek to help and serve others with kindness, gentleness, and love. It is God's intention that our salvation will result in acts of service to others. As His children in Christ, we belong to Him. We are His masterpiece, His workmanship, His work of art. Since this is true, we dare not treat ourselves or others with disrespect or as inferior work.

80 ⟶ **"For He made Him who had no sin to be sin for us, that we might become the righteousness of God in Him."**
2 Corinthians 5:21

This verse has been referred to as *The Great Exchange*. Without sufficient back ground in the Scriptures, it may be a little difficult to understand, but in essence it hits at the very core of the Gospel message. The "Good News" for all who will believe, simply, is that Jesus took our punishment so that we might receive His righteousness. The only way we can live eternally with our holy and righteous God is for us to be made holy and righteous ourselves; and the only way we can be made righteous and holy is through faith in God's Son. By dying on the cross for us, He paid our sin debt in full, and by doing so, the great exchange took place. He took our sins, including all the sins of the world, and in exchange He gave us His righteousness and sinless nature. What an exchange that was! It was all in our favor. In modern language, we got the best end of the deal! Just think, it was all free! We didn't have to do anything other than accept it as a gift. Jesus did it all! He suffered and died that we might live. He went to hell in our place so that we could live in heaven with our holy and righteous God. But that's not the end of the story. The rest of the story is that God raised His Son from the dead, and He lived on earth for another forty days before He ascended into heaven where He is now seated at the right hand of God the Father (see Hebrews 10:12). The further good news is that all Christians, meaning all those of us who trust in Christ and His great exchange, will also be raised from the dead and have everlasting life with Him. Now that's what I call really good news!

81 〜 "Therefore, having been justified by faith, we have peace with God through our Lord Jesus Christ." Romans 5:1

When Paul tells us we have been "justified by faith," he's telling us we have been made right in God's sight by our faith in what Jesus did for us on the cross. This is called the *doctrine of justification,* which is a basic principle of the Christian faith. Amazingly enough, I went to church all my life, but never heard it preached until I became serious about studying God's Word. When we accept Christ by faith, we are justified, which means we have been made right with God. To be right with God means we have *peace with God.* To have peace with God does not necessarily mean we have *the peace of God*—which has to do with peaceful feelings such as calmness and tranquility. There is an important distinction between the two. When we place our faith in the risen Christ and are made right with God, the war with heaven is over. We move from darkness to light. We are no longer enemies of God—we become His beloved children. We move from death to life and therefore God begins to shower His peace and blessings upon those who trust Him. *Peace with God* means we have been reconciled with Him. There is no longer any hostility between us—there's no sin blocking our relationship with Him. The key to our having peace is Jesus. Because He paid the price for our sins through His death on the cross, we are "justified by faith." The doctrine of justification sets in motion the doctrine of sanctification which is the subject of the next Scripture. Read on, because it is essential to Christian growth and becoming the child of God we were designed to be.

82 ⮞ **"For by one offering He has perfected those who are be-ing sanctified." Hebrews 10:14**

After we are justified and made right with God through our faith in His Son Jesus, God sets in motion what theologians calls the *doctrine of sanctification*. As with the doctrine of justification, I don't remember having heard much about the doctrine of sanctification growing up. I had vaguely heard the phrase, but I knew nothing about its meaning until much later in my Christian walk. Although there are deeper meanings connected with the doctrine as a whole, the basic concept is that sanctification is a process. When we receive Christ, we are justified and made righteous. That is our position in the eyes of our holy God. And yet at the same time, from a practical point of view, we are in the process of being made holy. This process is called sanctification. We might say that in *position* we are holy, but in *practice* we are being made holy. As our heavenly Father, God is progressively cleansing His children and setting us apart for His special use in our daily pilgrimage. This is a lifelong process while we continue to live out our earthly existence. We can refer to it as "Christian growth" or "growing in Christ." In other words, when we are justified by faith, God is not finished with us. His number one purpose for each of His children is that we be conformed to the image and likeness of His Son. With Jesus as our perfect example, God wants us to go through the process of becoming more like Him each day. We can encourage this growth by accepting and applying the discipline and guidance Christ provides. Our objective should be to give Him total control of our desires and goals. Sanctification is a lifelong process. Our livelong goal of being conformed to the image and likeness of Jesus will be complete only when our work on earth is done and we meet our Savior face to face in heaven. Then we will be in the perfect image and likeness of Jesus.

83 ⮞ **"To them God willed to make known what are the riches of the glory of this mystery among the gentiles: which is Christ in you, the hope of glory." Colossians 1:27**

God had a special assignment in mind for Saul of Tarsus, when Saul had the experience of meeting Jesus on the road to Damascus. God changed

Saul's name to Paul and gave him a passion and responsibility for serving His Church by proclaiming His Gospel message. This message had been kept secret for centuries and generations past, but now was about to be revealed to His people. God wanted them to know that the riches and glory of Christ are also for the gentiles. In Old Testament times, the Holy Spirit came upon His chosen people to enable them to do God's will at certain times for a specific purpose. He came upon them, but never actually took up residence in them as believers as He does today. And that was the mystery or secret God had planned since before the foundation of the world. He had in mind that His Son, Jesus Christ, in the form of the Holy Spirit, would live in the hearts of all who believed in Him. That meant every believer, whether Jew or Greek, black or white, male or female, free or slave. That truth is for us today, whether we as believers recognize it or not. It took me a long time after I accepted Christ at the age of twelve to discover that "mystery" within my own life. In fact, I call that *my greatest discovery* as referred to in my book of the same title. I pray the indwelling Christ will be the discovery of every believer. Bear in mind, Christ does not take up residence in a nonbeliever. You must accept Jesus as your Lord and Savior for Him to dwell in you. But once you do, it is a simultaneous act of God. The moment you truly believe is the moment the Spirit of Christ Jesus comes into your heart in the form of the Holy Spirit. If you are a believer, I pray you will discover, "Christ in you, the hope of glory." Once that discovery is made, He will change your life as He changed mine.

84 ⟶ **"For as many as are led by the Spirit of God, these are sons of God." Romans 8:14**

Once we become a child of God, His Holy Spirit permanently indwells us. Jesus was (and is) the only begotten Son of God, because it was the Holy Spirit Himself who impregnated the Virgin Mary. She gave physical birth to the second Person of the Trinity—Jesus Christ, who was the only begotten Son of God. That's why Jesus is known as the God-Man, the incarnate God, and God in the flesh. God wants to lead us and be the "Polar Star" for all of His children. For that reason, He provided the third Person of the Trinity, the indwelling Holy Spirit, to be our guide as we walk with Him, day by day and year by year, until His work for us on earth is done. The Bible says that the purpose of the Holy Spirit is to be our Counselor, our Helper, and our Comforter, and to lead us into all truth. Our job is to let Him have his way with us by yielding to His leading. We learn "The Power of Letting" by developing an intimate relationship with our heavenly Father. We can't emphasize too strongly that the best way to have an intimate relationship with God is to spend *sufficient quality time* in His presence — by meditating on His Word, in prayer, praise, and thanksgiving for who He is and for His faithfulness in providing for our every need. To be led by the Spirit should be the goal of every Christian. My greatest desire is to yield to His leading, so as to let Him have His way with my life. As Jesus said, "Not My will but Thine be done."

85 ∽ "For if we live, we live to the Lord; and if we die, we die to the Lord. Therefore, whether we live or die, we are the Lord's." Romans 14:8

Many times we hear this and the following verse preached at funerals. Verse 9 continues, "For to this end Christ died and rose and lived again, that He might be Lord of both the dead and the living." The *New Living Translation* puts a little different slant on the meaning of verse 8, "If we live, it's to honor the Lord. And if we die, it's to honor the Lord. So whether we live or die, we belong to the Lord." What does Paul mean when he tells us that, "We are the Lord's" or "We belong to the Lord?" In the context of the whole passage, he's making it clear that we are God's children and we should honor Him as our heavenly Father in life and in death. I remember my daddy telling me, as well as Warren and Ely, when we would go out and not be in his presence, "Remember who you belong to. You belong to your Mama and Daddy." That was before he knew Christ in a real way. It was just Daddy's way of telling his children that we belonged to Mama and him and we should act like it. I remember that each time he said it, it was indeed a reminder that everything I did would reflect on my upbringing and the training I had received while living under their roof. Interestingly enough, Daddy's words were not spoken only when I would leave home for some reason. Many times just out of the clear blue, for no particular reason, while I was playing on the floor or just sitting around looking at a Superman funny book, he would interrupt with the question, "Who do you belong to, young man?" That was his way of preparing me for life's greater lesson: that as a Christian, everything we do should be a reflection on the Savior who bought us with His own blood. Even the way we die should be a witness to Jesus Christ, for every moment of every day we belong to Him.

86 ～ "Teach me Your ways, O Lord, that I may live according to Your truth! Grant me purity of heart, so that I may honor You" Psalms 86:11 (NLT).

This is a prayer of David that should be adopted by all of us who are serious about our walk with the Lord. Notice that in this single verse, David is making two requests: (1) "Teach me Your ways," and (2) "Grant me purity of heart." Why does David want the Lord to teach him His ways? Because David's desire is to "live according to Your truth." In today's world, this should be the goal of all of us who claim to be Christians. We have the Holy Spirit living within us. His job is to "lead us into all truth," and He will do that if we will but yield to His leading. How do we yield ourselves? By purposing in our heart through daily prayer to, "Teach me Your ways, O Lord, that I may live according to Your truth." But look at the second part of David's model prayer which says, "Grant me purity of heart, so that I may honor You." David knew that his heart had to be right with God for God to honor his prayer. That should be our prayer, that our hearts will be pure so that we can honor God. It is through a pure heart that our heavenly Father can effectively communicate with us as His children through the power of the Holy Spirit. Accordingly, Paul advised young Timothy, "If you keep yourself pure, you will be a special utensil for honorable use. Your life will be clean, and you will be ready for the Master to use you for every good work" (2 Timothy 2:21) (NLT). Jesus Himself echoed His approval in the sixth beatitude: "Blessed are the pure in heart, for they shall see God" (Matthew 5:6). A model prayer for all of us is: *Lord, teach us Your ways that we may live according to Your truth. Grant us purity of heart, so that we may honor You, in Jesus name. Amen.*

87 ~ "O God, You are my God; Early will I seek You; My soul thirsts for You; My flesh longs for You in a dry and thirsty land where there is no water." Psalms 63:1

Biblical scholars think that Psalms 61, 62, and 63 were probably written when David was seeking refuge during his son Absalom's rebellion. Many of us can identify with David as he is crying out to the Lord. He has already lived a full life. He has known the Lord and called upon Him in so many situations when he was facing enemies and other adversities such as when he was fleeing and hiding from King Saul. In his jealous rage, Saul was chasing David with one purpose in mind, to kill him. Most of us may not have had to contend with such plights as David faced, yet we all have adversities in our lives that greatly concern us. The question is how do we respond to such adversities? God has the answer to any and all of our problems. David's attitude can be a model for us to emulate. Can we claim that God is "my God?" Do we seek Him "early" and pursue Him throughout the day? Does our soul "thirst" for Him? Does our "flesh long for" Him all day long as David did? Most of us probably feel satisfied with an hour or two on Sunday. After all, being a "Sunday Christian" seems to be the norm for most of us. But the problem with being only a nominal Christian is we miss out on developing our relationship with our Lord and Savior who loves us with an undying love. He wants us to grasp the truth about His majesty, His holiness, His power, His love, His grace, and His joy. When we begin to comprehend these mighty truths about the person of God, we find ourselves enriched, enabled, and energized. If you are lonely or thirsty for something lasting in your life, remember David's prayer. I'm convinced along with David that God alone can satisfy your deepest longings.

88 ~ "He who dwells in the secret place of the Most High shall abide under the shadow of the Almighty." Psalms 91:1

When trouble comes into our lives, all of us need some place to go and some person to trust to help us get through the hard times. We need to find rest and peace in the midst of turmoil. The psalmist goes on to proclaim in verse 2 that, "I will say to the Lord, 'He is my refuge and my fortress; My God, in

Him I will trust.'" The writer of the psalm learned what all of us need to learn: the place we go to in time of trouble is, "the secret place of the Most High" and the person we can trust in is "the Almighty"—the God of the universe. We Christians call Him "our heavenly Father." The *secret* place referred to can be any physical place, but it must be a place where we can "abide under the shadow of the Almighty." It must be a place where we can have uninterrupted communion with the Almighty God. Verse 1 of the *New Living Translation* reads, "Those who live in the shelter of the Most High will find rest in the shadow of the Almighty." We need to understand and truly learn that God is our shelter and refuge when we are afraid. It is He who is our protector to carry us through all the dangers and fears of life. Psalm 91:1 gives us a picture of our trust in Him, no matter how intense our fears. Our objective should be to trade all our fears for faith in Him. My friend, Sammy Hudson, sets a good example for us all by his lifestyle of faith and trust as executive director of the Refuge, a budding ministry that seeks to provide such a "secret place of the Most High." His passion is personally to abide under the shadow of the Almighty and then to provide a "secret place" for others to experience the abiding refuge "in the shelter of the Most High."

89 ∽ "So then faith comes from hearing, and hearing by the Word of God." Romans 10:17

The central message of Romans 10 is found in the first verse: "Brethren, my heart's desire and prayer to God for Israel is that they may be saved." This is the longing of Paul's heart. As a Jew himself, Paul (formerly Saul) had not met the risen Savior and was saved by God's grace through his faith during his Damascus Road experience. He knew the meaning and blessing that came to him, and now he wanted his fellow Jews to experience the same salvation. In verses 2 and 3, he explains, "They have zeal for God, but not according to knowledge." He goes on to say, "For they being ignorant of God's righteousness and seeking to establish their own righteousness, have not submitted to the righteousness of God." In verse 4, Paul gives the bottom line: "For Christ is the end of the law for righteousness of God." Then in verse 9, he gives the

Good News: "If you confess with your mouth the Lord Jesus and believe in your heart that God raised Him from the dead, you will be saved." Everything anyone needs to know about our salvation from the penalty of sin is found in the Word of God. The problem is most of us don't take the time to read it so as to find out what the Good news of salvation is all about. Why does every person living on this earth—whether Jew, Gentile, black, white, rich, or poor—why do we all need salvation? How can we receive it? It's all in God's Word, the Holy Bible. We are saved by God's grace through our faith in the risen Lord Jesus. So in verse 17, Paul sums it up by telling us that faith comes from hearing the Good News about Christ *as explained in the Word of God.*

90 ⁓ **"Therefore, if anyone is in Christ, he is a new creation; old things have passed away; behold, all things have become new." 2 Corinthians 5:17**

This is more good news! In fact, everything about Christianity is good news. This verse is telling us that once we receive Christ and trust that He paid our sin debt for us, we are brand new people on the inside. Why? Because when we receive Christ we receive the Spirit of God, in the form of the Holy Spirit. He lives in every Christian. When we have the indwelling Holy Spirit, we are not the same as before, for we now have a new life. In the fourth chapter of his letter, Paul refers to a comparison between the *old man* and the *new man.* In essence, we have a new life under a new Master. We are now able to see life from a new perspective. In fact, under Christ's authority there is an entirely new order for all creation, which requires a new way of looking at all people as well as all of creation. The question for all Christians is, does our new life reflect this new perspective? Oh, but there's one catch! Just because we have the Holy Spirit indwelling us does not mean we are free from the vile influences of the flesh. The difference is, we now have the Holy Spirit to help us counteract those evil influences. The flesh is the avenue by which Satan can gain a stronghold in our lives, *if we allow him to do so.* Someone has said that the flesh is the landing field or runway on which Satan pilots his airplane to enter our lives. Our defense lies in appropriating the power of the Holy Spirit within us. Without Him, we are defenseless. We have no power to detect Satan's lies and withstand his attacks. We should be forever thankful that we are "a new creation" in Christ and that we have the indwelling Holy Spirit to lead us to victory over Satan.

91 ❧ **"I have been crucified with Christ; it is no longer I who live, but Christ lives in me; and the life I now live in the flesh I live by faith in the Son of God who loved me and gave Himself for me." Galatians 2:20**

The first question many of us would ask is how can Paul or "I" be crucified with Christ? Legally speaking, God looks at us his children as if we had died with Christ. We are no longer condemned, because our sins died with Him. Relationally speaking, we have become one with Christ and His experiences are our experiences. When our Christian life began, we died to our old life and we were united with Christ. In like manner, not only were we crucified with Him, but we also were raised with Him. Our old self died and we were given new life. So it is that our focus is not on dying, but on living. *The secret to the Christian life is to allow Christ to live His life in and through us.* That is why Paul can say, "It is no longer I who live, but Christ lives in me." In that sense we live our lives as representatives of Christ, and that's who we are when we allow the Holy Spirit to live and work in our lives. Paul makes it clear that we live out the Christian life through faith — by trusting in Jesus "who loved me and gave Himself for me." Because He indwells us, we are no longer alone. As we grow to understand His indwelling presence, we begin to sense that He is our power for living, and He is our hope for the future. What a powerful message for us to learn! The more we comprehend and are able to apply, "It is no longer I who live, but Christ lives in me," the more we are able to enjoy the blessings God gives us for living out who we are in Christ. We can take no credit. It's all Christ in us who does the work. That's a mystery that needs to be discovered by all of us who claim to be Christians.

92 ∽ "For the message of the cross is foolishness to those who are perishing, but to us who are being saved it is the power of God." 1 Corinthians 1:18

Why does Paul say that "the message of the cross is foolishness to those who are perishing?" It's a matter of understanding God's way as opposed to the world's way. The prophet Isaiah as well as Jesus Himself often emphasized that God's way of thinking is not like the world's way of thinking. "My thoughts are nothing like your thoughts," says the Lord. "And My ways are far beyond anything you could imagine. For just as the heavens are higher than the earth, so My ways are higher than your ways and My thoughts higher than your thoughts" (Isaiah 55:8-9) (NLT). God's wisdom and the world's wisdom are on two different levels and are in two different ballparks. God offers eternal life, which the world can never give. We can spend a lifetime accumulating worldly wisdom, and yet never learn to have a personal relationship with God. The message of the cross is the message of salvation through Jesus' death on the cross. It is given by God, and therefore the world cannot understand it. In fact, to the worldly thinker it is sheer foolishness. It doesn't make sense, because it is totally foreign to their way of thinking. Why does Paul say it is foolishness to those who are perishing? Because the world is perishing in that it does not know Jesus as its Lord and Savior. But, says Paul, to those who understand and are being saved, the message of the cross is "the power of God." Oh, that the world could understand and follow Christ rather than be ignorant of the cross and perish! Verse 22 says, "It is foolish to the Jews, who ask for signs from heaven. And it is foolish to the Greeks [Gentiles] who seek human wisdom" (NLT).

93 ∽ "Don't you realize that your body is the temple of the Holy Spirit, who lives in you and was given to you by God? You do not belong to yourself, . . ." 1 Corinthians 6:19 (NLT)

Most Christians have no problem with understanding that when you receive Christ by asking Him to come into your life, the Holy Spirit at that moment begins to indwell you. It is also easy to understand that Paul refers to the body as the "temple of the Holy Spirit." The Holy Spirit lives in your body and, in that sense, the body is the temple of the Holy Spirit. Likewise, we don't have any problem believing that the Holy Spirit is a gift of God, because His Spirit was "given to you by God." But it takes a little more maturity to understand the last phrase of the 19th verse, which reads, "You do not belong to yourself, . . ." A lot of women, in particular, both Christian as well as non-Christian, have a hard time with that thought. They reason that, "It's my body and I can do what I want to with it. If I want to have an abortion, I can do it." With that kind of thinking, no consideration is given to the fact that abortion spells murder. Notice that the verse, "You do not belong to yourself," ends with a comma. Verse 20 goes on to explain, "For God bought you with a high price. So you must honor God with your body." What was the high price He paid for us? Our heavenly Father sacrificed His own Son, Jesus the Christ, by sending Him to the cross to die for *us* and, thereby, to pay *our* sin debt. Christ's death freed us from sin, but it also obligated us to His service. Since our body belongs to God, we must not violate His standards for living. Paul further explains in his letter to the Romans: "And so dear brothers and sisters, I plead with you to give your bodies to God because of all He has done for you. Let them be a living and holy sacrifice—the kind He will find acceptable. This is truly the way to worship Him" (Rom. 12:1) (NLT). "A living and holy sacrifice" means to daily lay aside our own desires to follow Him and His desires. He wants us to put all our energy and resources at His disposal and to trust Him to guide us.

94 ∽ **"Do not be deceived, God is not mocked; for whatever a man sows, that he will also reap." Galatians 6:7**

I have heard Charles Stanley preach on this verse many times. His central message is, "You reap what you sow, more than you sow, and later than you sow." It's interesting to note that we are today what we have been thinking and the way we have lived in the past. The law of sowing and reaping is a principle that serves both as a warning and an encouragement. Stanley refers to it as an unalterable law that affects everyone, whether we are Christians or not, in every area of life—family, work, or pleasure. Every farmer understands this principle. He sows an apple seed and he expects to reap apples, not peaches.

He reaps what he sows. But he reaps more than he sows. He will harvest not just one apple, but many apples; and he will reap the many apples later than he sows the one. Some crops we reap quickly; others take a long time. Many believers live under a deceptive spirit, for they have a careless and indulgent lifestyle. Paul advises them, "Do not be deceived, God is not mocked." Amazingly enough their lifestyle reveals one of two things: They either do not believe the truth, or they think they will somehow be the exception to God's law. I daresay that most believers do, in fact, believe the truth of the law of sowing and reaping. *But they are deceived into thinking they will somehow be the exception to the rule.* They think they can fool God, but Paul makes it clear that, "God is not mocked." To mock God is to turn one's nose up at Him, in hopes they can outwit Him. What a foolish thought! They give little credence to the fact that "We must all appear before the judgment seat of Christ, that each one may receive the things done in the body, according to what he has done, whether good or bad" (2 Cor. 5:10). The question for all of us is, what kind of seeds are we sowing? Are they for our eventual good or bad? Will they enhance our relationship with the Lord or weaken it?

95   "For I am not ashamed of the gospel of Christ, for it is the power of God to salvation for everyone who believes, for the Jew first and also for the Greek." Romans 1:16

In each of my three previous books, I have always referenced Romans 1:16 after autographing the book for distribution to others. I had originally considered several other Scriptures, but settled on Romans 1:16 when Margaret suggested it suited my lifestyle more than any of the others. At first, I thought it would be undeserving and even bragging for me to claim that, "I am not ashamed of the gospel of Christ." Upon deeper reflection and prayer, I felt the Lord was telling me that there was a time in my life that I was indeed hesitant to even mention the name of Jesus openly and freely, much less witness the gospel message to others. Not that I was *ashamed* of the gospel — it just wasn't the thing to do. I guess I thought I would be considered weird or some kind of religious fanatic. But over a period of years, as I began to examine and study God's Word, He made it clear that He wanted me to stand up for the truth of

His Word. I was not to be ashamed of the gospel, but to boldly proclaim it. He let me know that if I was willing to proclaim the gospel, He would lead me and show me how He wanted me to do it. My response was and still is, "Okay, Lord, I'm willing to be led. Please show me what and how you want me to do." One of the avenues He has shown me is through writing. I realize I'm not the best in the world at expressing myself or the message that He gives me. All I do is try to put down on paper what I feel He is leading me to write. The gospel message is "the power of God to salvation." It is too critically important a message to be ashamed of.

96 ∾ "For it is written: 'As I live, says the Lord, every knee shall bow to Me, and every tongue shall confess to God.'" Romans 14:11

Here Paul is quoting the Old Testament prophet as written in Isaiah 45:23. In the context of Paul's writing, he is saying that there will come a time when every knee will bow before the Lord God and every tongue will confess to Him that Jesus Christ is God and the Lord of all life. That time is coming whether we believe it or not. The Bible teaches that each person is accountable to Christ and not to one another. In today's society, many Christians tend to base their moral judgments on personal opinions and dislikes. Personal and cultural bias in many instances has become the basis for judicial decisions in the highest courts in the land. In the early years of our country, the Word of God reigned supreme. In these modern days, it is the biased flexibility of man's opinion rather than the enduring stability of God's Word that is the prevailing sign of the times. For the unbeliever and those who doubt that Jesus is who He claimed to be, the truth will rise to the surface in God's perfect timing. John records these words of Jesus in talking to his disciples: "It is the Spirit who gives life; the flesh profits nothing. The words that I speak to you are spirit, and they are life" (John 6:63). Then He tells them something that widely holds true today: "But there are some of you who do not believe." Yes, there are some of us who are churchgoers and have heard the Word preached, but still do not believe. They may believe "a little here and there," but they've never believed enough to accept Jesus as their Lord and

Savior and to live their lives for Him. But we can all rest assured that there will come a day, as the Scripture proclaims, "That at the name of Jesus every knee shall bow, of those who are in heaven, and of those on earth, and that every tongue shall confess that Jesus Christ is Lord, to the Glory of God the Father" (Philippians 2:10-11).

97 ⟶ **"Trust in the Lord with all your heart, and lean not on your own understanding; in all your ways acknowledge Him, and He shall direct your paths." Proverbs 3:5-6**

This passage has had special meaning for me for a long time, but especially over the past ten years or so. I have increasingly come to realize that the power of the Christian walk comes from allowing the indwelling Holy Spirit to have His way with me. The more I cooperate with His leading, the more true joy I find in living each day. When Solomon began his reign as king of Israel, God invited him to ask for whatever he wanted. He could have asked for riches and power, but he chose "an understanding heart to judge Your people that I may discern between good and evil . . ." (1 Kings 3:9). Through his God-given wisdom, Solomon learned that only a fool tries to solve life's problems without God's help. No one goes through this life without trials and tests. These adversities come in all shapes and sizes. Some we can anticipate; others require us to make the right decision immediately. It makes no difference how the package is wrapped, God instructs us to trust Him and not to rely on our own understanding. In the words of the psalmist, "It is better to trust in the Lord than to put confidence in man. It is better to trust in the Lord than to put confidence in princes" (Psalms 118:8-9). For some of us this may be a hard lesson to learn, especially in politics. We tend to want to do the will of the people. It takes no genius to realize that man's way is steadily leading us away from the truth of God's Word. The wise person will not only read and reread Proverbs 3:5 and 6, but he will, through prayer and meditation, seek to follow Solomon's wise instruction to "Trust in the Lord with all your heart, and lean not on your own understanding; In all your ways acknowledge Him, and He will direct your path."

98 ∽ "... they received the Word with all readiness and searched the Scriptures daily to find out whether these things were so." Acts 17:11

This verse is the central theme of the Berean Call Ministry and should be the standard for evaluating all sermons and teachings. The people of Berea sought to verify the message they heard preached by searching the Scriptures for themselves. They set the example for all of us. In other words, we should always compare what we hear with what the Bible says. When Randy Spaugh began his ministry in Kinston, one of the first things he said was that he may not be right in everything he preaches. If something he says doesn't quite ring true in the ears of the believer, then we should go back to the Word of God and compare what Randy says with what the Bible says. A preacher or teacher who gives God's true message will never contradict or explain away anything that's found in God's Word. I frankly don't remember ever having to test Randy's preaching with biblical truth. This is not the case with some other teachers I've heard, both on television and in person. Sometimes it's an obvious error. Other times require a thorough search of the Scriptures to see exactly what the Bible says as compared to what was said from the pulpit or elsewhere. I'm convinced that the Bible is the inerrant, infallible Word of God and it can be trusted. That's another thing Randy often says after he reads the morning Scripture. He lets it be known that "This is the Word of God, and it can be trusted." I find it very comforting to realize that the Sovereign God of the universe has given us a plumb line as a basis for all truth. We should follow the example of the Bereans as they "searched the Scriptures daily."

99 ∽ "This is the day the Lord has made; we will rejoice and be glad in it." Psalm 118:24

This was my brother Warren's favorite verse of Scripture, and he was not afraid to let it be known. At Rotary Club meetings, when he was asked to give the blessing for the food, he would quite often have us all hold hands and raise them above our heads, saying together Psalm 118:24 before offering his prayer. His boldness in proclaiming his joy in the Lord was contagious among his fellow Rotarians, as well as in other groups. When the Perry family gathers at the Fun Farm or in our homes to share a meal that calls for a blessing for the food, most of the time we continue that tradition started by Warren. He left his earthly existence to begin his eternal life with Jesus on June 16, 2003. Since that time, I've had many people tell me what a great witness that tradition has been to them. One of the translations says, "Let us rejoice and be glad in it." Whether we say "Let us rejoice" or "We will rejoice," the message is the same. The psalmist is conveying the thought that we are to rejoice because the day was made and given to us by the Lord. Our response should be to *rejoice and be glad* in each of our God-given days. But what if it's one of our "bad days?" What if our mood is down because we are experiencing some overwhelming sorrow? There are times when the natural man questions, *Rejoice? That's the last thing I want to do is rejoice! How can I rejoice and be glad for the situation I'm in and for what I'm going through?* Notice that the psalmist doesn't say to rejoice and be glad only when things are going well. He says to rejoice and be glad whether we think the day is good or bad. It's still the day the Lord has made, and we are to rejoice and be glad accordingly. I have found that it helps me when I don't feel like rejoicing in a time of trial and testing to tell God how I truly feel. As I begin to praise Him and thank Him for His many countless blessings, He gives me a reason to rejoice and be glad.

100   "And whatever you do, do it heartily as to the Lord, and not to men." Colossians 3:23

From time to time all of us experience disappointment and frustration in the things we do, whether it's in work, or play, whether it's doing something constructive or spending leisure time just "doing nothing." We may be the most devout of Christians and have the best intentions, but there are times when our minds are far from thinking about the Lord's work. Did Paul really mean to use the all inclusive word *whatever* when he said, "Whatever you do, do it heartily as to the Lord, and not to men." That's a real test for all of us, no matter who we are, and yet Paul is giving us a demanding challenge—at least something to shoot for. In 1 Corinthians 10:31, he presents the same idea, just worded a little differently: "Therefore, whether you eat or drink, or whatever you do, do all to the glory of God." Realistically speaking, we have a choice as to whom we will serve. We can grocery shop for Jesus or we can do it for a cranky husband. We can do our jobs for Christ or we can do them for a disrespectful supervisor. It's a matter of attitude. Since the beginning of time, God has given us work and chores to do. The Bible teaches that whatever we do, whether it's work or play, we should do it as an act of worship. It should be done as a service to God rather than to man. If we trust our various tasks as the cost of discipleship, we can do whatever we do without complaint or resentment. When I look at the lives of Jimbo Perry as a practicing attorney and Sammy Hudson as the director of The Refuge ministry, I see two prevailing attitudes as they approach their work: (1) each views himself as a servant, which reminds me of the adage, "Whoever wants to be a leader must adopt a servant attitude;" and (2) each realizes he is working for the Lord Himself. If Jesus Christ is our Lord and Savior, He is ultimately our employer and is always on site as our supervisor, whether we're at work or play. We cannot exclude Him from any part of our lives, for the indwelling Holy Spirit is ever present—equipping and energizing us to do His work in whatever we do, and to do it "heartily as to the Lord, and not to men."

101 ᘓ "And we know that all things work together for good to those who love God, to those who are called according to His purpose." Romans 8:28

As I come to the end of my most meaningful Bible verses, I am aware that it is almost impossible to say which is my favorite. If, on the other hand, I were forced to pick a favorite, it would have to be Romans 8:28. Why? Because the truth of its text is in the forefront of my mind most every day of my life. Charles Stanley has pointed out over the years that a better translation of the words, "all things work together for good" is "God *causes* all things to work together for good." The *New Living Translation,* along with several other translations, uses the word "causes" which has special meaning for me. The word "engineering" can also be used to indicate that God is in control.

Paul is not saying that everything that happens to us is good. But he is saying that even though evil and adverse situations are prevalent in our fallen world, God is able to turn every circumstance around for our long-range good. He's causing and even engineering them to work out for our good. Notice that this promise is not for everyone. It can be claimed only for "those who love God" and are "called according to His purpose." He is referring to those who are called by Him. The footnote says, "Those whom the Holy Spirit convinces to receive Christ." These are people who are saved by God's grace through their faith in Jesus. They have a new perspective and a new mindset. Their trust is in God and not in their worldly treasures. In other words, their security is in heaven and not on earth. They have confidence in the fact that God is not only with them, but He also indwells them in the form of the Holy Spirit. The question for you and me is, do we have faith that God does not waiver in His faithfulness to us during our pain and persecution? Can we bank on the fact that God not only can, but also does in fact, *cause all things* to work together for our good—if we love Him and are called according to His purpose? The Bible makes it clear that ". . . His ways are everlasting" (Habakkuk 3:6), and that "Jesus Christ is the same yesterday, today and forever" (Hebrews 13:8). What an assurance this is for all believers in Jesus Christ! Our triune God does not change. His faithfulness endures forever!

CONCLUSION

So there you have it! *101 Quirks, Quips, and Quotes* that include fifty-six of my crazy sayings, fourteen meaningful thoughts that have played a significant role in my life, and thirty-one of my favorite Bible verses that have special meaning to me. It is my hope that the reader will have gained at least token insight into the lighthearted nature of my personality, as well as the serious side of my belief system. Above all, I want people to know who I am, what I believe in, and what I stand for.

Dan E. Perry
March 2010

Dan and Margaret
Sweethearts and best friends for 47 years

Made in the USA
Columbia, SC
26 May 2023

17340429R00057